The Elysian Bridge

The Elysian Bridge

DJ DONOVAN

authorHOUSE®

AuthorHouse™ LLC
1663 Liberty Drive
Bloomington, IN 47403
www.authorhouse.com
Phone: 1-800-839-8640

Published by AuthorHouse   04/16/2014

ISBN: 978-1-4969-0646-5 (sc)
ISBN: 978-1-4969-0718-9 (e)

Bless'd in Wife
Bless'd in Life

Dedicated to Margaret, the best wife I could ever imagine having.

Dave

People plant a garden with the seeds they are given.
Some gardens produce an abundance of vegetables
and not a few beautiful flowers.
Others produce an abundance of weeds, a few
vegetables, and maybe some scraggly flowers.
You see, it isn't the seeds you plant. It is how
you tend the garden that counts.

Elysium
Elysian plain (plain of the departed).
"The dwelling place of virtuous people after death."
"Any place or condition of ideal bliss or complete happiness: Paradise."
Webster's New World Dictionary

CHAPTER

1

Elaine pulled on her boots and buttoned her coat. As she walked across the barnyard, she listened, expecting her mother to yell at her to stay out of the barn. Roberta was watching her from the kitchen window, smiling to herself. She wanted to see if Elaine would go into the barn by herself. She was usually with her father, Nathan, and he had told her not to go there alone.

Elaine walked right in and stopped just inside the door. She loved the smell of the hay and straw stored there, along with the smell of the cows and calves penned there. She used to be afraid because the barn was dimly lit and the hay was piled up in some places to the rafters, high above the loft. She walked under the loft to the pens where the cows and their newborn calves were. She liked to stand outside the pens and reach through the boards to pet the calves. She knew not to go inside, because the cows were huge and Daddy had told her she could get stepped on. Then her mother came in behind her and said, "Elaine, you are not supposed to be in here alone. Didn't your father tell you to wait until he could come in here with you?"

Elaine just smiled at Mommy and said, "He told me not to go in the pen with the cows, so I thought it would be all right to come in if I stayed outside the pen."

Roberta just shook her head and tried not to laugh. "What am I going to do with you? You are only four years old, and if you got stepped on, we would have to take you to the hospital."

Elaine said, "Mommy, I don't go into the pen even when Daddy is with me."

Roberta just shook her head and said, "Well, we need to gather the eggs, so let's get it done before lunch. Your father will be back anytime now."

Elaine loved the barn and the animals, but she didn't care much for the chickens. She held the basket while her mother took the eggs out of the nests. She didn't like reaching under the hens to see if there were eggs under them. She liked following her father around while he worked. She had been doing that since she was big enough to keep up. She loved going up into the loft when he was bringing bales of hay down to the cows. There was a huge pair of doors that opened out at the end of the barn, where they used a conveyor to load the hay into the barn after it was baled. When her daddy worked up there, he would open the doors to let the breeze blow through. Elaine would stand and look out over the farm. It was her favorite place to watch everything going on down below.

As Elaine grew older, feeding the cows and calves became one of her chores. By the time she started grade school, she was helping with everything she could handle. But most of all, she loved the garden. Nathan and Roberta always had a large garden. They raised nearly all of their own food. As Elaine grew older, she gradually took charge of the garden. She had started by helping her mom and dad, but each year as she learned, more and more her parents found that she was a step ahead of them in planning what she wanted to put in each year. Nathan plowed and disced the ground for her, but Elaine planted and weeded and sprayed for insects. When the vegetables were ready, she picked them and helped with canning them for the winter. The truth was, even though she didn't realize it, she loved being outside working more than being inside playing.

She was a nature lover. She knew the names of every animal—wild or domestic—on the farm. When it came to sewing or needlework, she left that to Mom or her grandmother. She couldn't sit still that long, and being inside was just too confining. Nathan's dad had died when Elaine was a baby, and her grandmother lived with her sons and daughter, moving every few months so her children took turns having her. Elaine loved it when she was with them. Grandma would tell her what it was like when she was a young girl on the farm while she was sitting there knitting afghans or crocheting doilies for her children.

Elaine did like to cook. There was just something about preparing food from the vegetables she had raised herself.

As she grew older, she would sneak out at night in the summer when the moon was full and go down to the pasture where her dad kept a salt block for the cows, and she would watch for an occasional deer to show up. On moonless nights she liked to lie outside and look up into the heavens. She wondered at it all. Where did it end, and if it did, what was beyond the end? Her parents had taken her to Sunday school and taught her about the Bible and religion when she was little, but she was still not sure what she believed. She knew she believed in God. How else could you explain the heavens and the natural world around you? When she started high school, she studied all of the things she wondered about. She realized how little was known about the very world she lived in.

She was becoming a real beauty, and boys were attracted to her like a magnet. She really wasn't interested. She thought about boys, but for some reason the ones she knew didn't appeal to her. She went to the proms and occasionally on a date, but only with someone she was comfortable being with.

In her junior year of high school she began to be interested in bookkeeping and accounting and business. She had made the connection between farming and business. Like everything else she did, she jumped in with a passion. Soon she was keeping the books for the farm and started talking to her dad about investing. Along with her parents, she had been saving money for college, and she understood before they did that where you saved that money made a difference. By the time she started college, they had built a pretty nice nest egg for her. She would have stayed at home and attended a local college, but her parents wanted her to experience living away from home. She understood their feelings, but she really would have preferred staying home. None of them could have foreseen what the decision to go away to college would mean to them all.

CHAPTER

2

Ed Williams was feeding pigs and chickens as soon as he was big enough to carry a bucket. His dad farmed a couple of hundred acres of his own and rented another hundred or so from neighbors who were getting too old to do the work themselves. Ed didn't think much about whether he really liked farming or not; it was just what was expected of him. He didn't dislike it he knew that his parents needed all the help they could get to do the work. As soon as he was big enough to drive the tractor, he was helping with the plowing and harvesting and everything in between. He realized at some point that his dad loved farming and was good at it, and that was enough for Ed.

Personally, he liked working on the equipment better than the actual farming. He was pretty good with his hands, and anything he undertook he did well. Nothing mechanical was too complicated for him. He would send off for a manual from the manufacturer and read through it until he understood how the machine operated. Once he started taking care of the machinery, his dad was amazed at how little trouble they had with it.

By the time Ed was in his junior year of high school, he knew he didn't really want to farm. He took a real interest in business and accounting. He started keeping the books for the farm, and he had a knack for reading and understanding all the tax schedules, so his dad pretty much left it to him.

When his father started talking about college, Ed didn't really want to go, but his parents finally convinced him that he should at least give it a try. His dad put it to him pretty bluntly. He knew Ed didn't really like to farm, and there were plenty of possible professions he would be exposed to in college. Maybe he could figure out what he did want to do.

If he didn't farm, he was going to have to learn to support himself with something. When Ed visited the college that appealed to him and read some of the curricula they offered, he realized right away that something in accounting would interest him. He thought he might become a certified public accountant or do something in business administration.

Also, the thought of living on campus and having to make all of his own decisions would be . . . well . . . liberating. It would also give him a chance to meet people from different backgrounds than his, and there would be lots of women. He had dated several girls in high school, but he had never found one he wanted to go steady with. They all just seemed to be so immature.

Ed was in his senior year of college when he walked into the bookstore and his life changed forever. He turned a corner and literally ran into the most beautiful girl he had ever seen. He knocked the books out of her hands, and was embarrassed and apologizing and making himself look like a fool. She just laughed and said it was all right, she was okay, and not to worry about it. Then she held out her hand and said, "Hi, my name is Elaine." He introduced himself and apologized again. Then, gathering his composure, he asked her if he could buy her lunch. He was pretty surprised when she accepted.

From that day on, they met every day that their class schedules would permit. They had dinner together every evening. They were like two peas in a pod. They were both farm kids, and they pretty much had the same interests. They were both surprised to learn that they were both pursuing degrees in accounting. She had gotten interested in accounting by keeping the books for her father's farm. Interestingly, they had grown up a few miles from each other but had never met. Both of their fathers were farmers, and they had both worked on the farms from the time they were big enough to help with the chores. They had grown up in different school districts, so they had never met.

Ed could never put his finger on what it was that was so different about Elaine. She had a way about her that defied description. Everyone was comfortable in her presence, and she had a way of bringing out the good in people. She was just a person that you liked to be around. After dating for a few weeks, they moved into an apartment, much to the disapproval of their parents. But it was obvious even to their parents that this was a match made in heaven. They were married at the end of their senior year, and after graduation, with a little help from their parents, they started Williams Accounting.

Elaine took on all roles in the business, from receptionist to accountant. The business did really well, in large part because they both worked however many hours it took to get things done. When she got pregnant with Michael, they were just reaching a point where they could hire some help and they could both concentrate on accounting. At first she thought she would just get her mother to babysit for her, or even bring Michael to work with her. Then she and Ed had a long sit-down, and she said if he could swing it, she would like to stay home with Michael until he started school. It was going to slow down the growth of the business, but Ed kind of liked the idea of her being home with Michael. So they hired a receptionist, and things seemed to be operating pretty well. Then three years later they had Teresa, and Elaine decided she would just have to put off working full time until both kids were in school. She still helped with the business, working part time at home. She also helped with a few charitable projects in the community when she had time.

CHAPTER

3

The clock radio came on at 6:30 a.m. Ed rolled over, shut it off, and rolled back over. Next to him Elaine said, "Oh, no, you don't! Feet on the floor! You told me to be sure you got going this morning. You have to deliver that report to Merrill Industries this morning. Head for the shower. I'll have breakfast on the table in twenty minutes." Ed roused up and headed for the bathroom. It had been seven years since they had started their accounting business, and an account with Merrill Industries would really put them on a solid financial footing. A month ago they had been contacted to do some work for Merrill Industries, the largest firm in Granville. This morning he would be delivering the report, and he hoped this would be just the first of many jobs for them.

Elaine thought about Ed as she was fixing breakfast. He was carrying the load at the office, and she could tell that it was wearing him down. He was completely worn out when he got home in the evenings. She was thinking about finding day care for the kids and getting back to the office. She could lighten his load, and she had to admit that she missed working with him. She had always liked her profession, even when they were working sixteen-hour days and still having trouble keeping up. Maybe after she finished shopping she would look into the day care idea.

The smell of coffee spurred Ed on, and he was walking into the kitchen just as she poured it and set his breakfast on the table. They talked as he ate, and they could hear the kids starting to stir, so she went in to help them get dressed. By the time he had eaten, they were in the kitchen and ready for breakfast. As he was getting ready to leave, Elaine got up to kiss him good-bye and the kids were holding up their arms for hugs. "What are you doing today?" he asked her.

"Shopping," she said. "We are going to the grocery, and I might stop by the mall and look at some clothes for Michael. He is growing out of everything."

He kissed her and the kids, gave them a hug, and was on his way.

CHAPTER

4

Ed stopped for lunch after leaving Merrill's, and he had just gotten back to the office when the receptionist came in and said, "There are two men here to see you, and I think one of them is a policeman!"

"Send them in," he said. As soon as they walked into his office, he was alarmed. The look on their faces was grave. "What's wrong?" he asked, almost afraid of the answer.

One of them stepped forward and said, "I'm Lieutenant Robertson from the Granville PD. I am sorry to have to bring you this news, but your wife and children were in an accident in town about an hour ago. They were hit by a dump truck when its brakes failed."

Ed was standing now and said, "Where are they now?"

The lieutenant replied, "They are at Granville Medical. I'm sorry, but they didn't survive."

Ed dropped into his chair. He felt numb. "I have to see them," he said. "This can't be; they were just going to the grocery store."

The other gentleman stepped forward and said, "I'm the hospital chaplain, and if you would like, we can take you over there. There are some arrangements that will have to be made. Is there someone we could call to come and help?"

"Call my parents," Ed said, "and Elaine's. My God, what am I going to do?"

The lieutenant asked, "Do you have their phone numbers?"

"I can't think. Ask my receptionist," Ed said.

The following week was just a blur. After the funeral all he could do was sit at home and cry. His parents stayed with him for a week. He was inconsolable. His mother sat down with him and told him, "We can't leave you alone here like this. Why don't you come home with us? It can't be good for you to stay here in this house alone."

In the end he moved back in with his parents and sold the house. He went through the motions at work, but he was having a difficult time concentrating. He found himself thinking about Elaine and the kids, and the pain was indescribable. He was making ridiculous mistakes, and he had even sent a tax return that wasn't finished to a client. Fortunately, most of his customers knew what had happened, and they tried to work with him to get things straightened out. Sometimes in the middle of something he was working on, he would think he needed to finish it later because he had to get home. He didn't want to keep Elaine and the kids waiting for dinner. Then everything would spin out of control, and he would have to close his eyes and will himself to get a grip on reality.

Then there were the horrible nightmares. Ed was riding in the passenger's seat, and Elaine was driving. He heard the honking of horns and looked up just in time to see the truck as it plowed into the driver's side of the car. He could hear the screech of metal and the beginnings of screams; he heard muffled sounds from the backseat. He bolted upright in bed in a cold sweat. He was shaking all over. He got out of bed and staggered to the bathroom and took a cold shower. The nightmares were starting to occur more often. He was going to have to do something. He thought about getting some kind of therapy, but in the end he just decided he had to get away from it all. He was trying to live a life that no longer existed.

After about six months of this, he sold the business because he just couldn't function in it. Maybe if he just helped on the farm, he would find himself on solid ground again. He thought that somehow he could bring back the normal feelings he'd had before he left for college. He plunged into the farm work with abandon, but he was just going through the motions. His father had to watch him to make sure he was getting everything done right, and after a few months his dad and mom decided it was time for a serious talk. His dad started, "Look," he said, "we have watched you beating yourself up over this for the last several months, and it can't go on."

His mother started to cry and added, "You aren't the only one suffering a loss here. We have lost our daughter-in-law and our grandchildren, whom we dearly loved. Now we feel like we are losing you as well. You wander around here all day, and you're up for half the night. You have got to pull yourself together and move on with your life. We love having you here helping with the farm, but I cry every night when I say my prayers because I can't stand to see what you are doing to yourself."

Ed sat in silence for a while, and then he said, "I don't know what to do. I know you're right, and I am really sorry, but I feel lost for the first time in my life. I have always known where I was going and what to do next, but now I'm clueless about what to do."

His dad took over the conversation. "I want you to get a job—preferably something that will occupy your mind—and then bury yourself in work. Eventually, this will pass. The pain will still be there, but it will become manageable."

Ed knew they were right, and the next week he rented an apartment in Granville and started looking for work.

The thought of taking up accounting and getting back into that line of work was too reminiscent of what he was trying to forget. He had sent out his resumes, and when he got a reply from the Merrill Homeless Shelter, he went in for an interview. He hadn't even known there was a shelter before he started looking for work. The shelter was a private charity, financed and run by Merrill Industries. They hired him on the spot. They knew he was overqualified, but what they needed was someone to act as a purchasing agent for all of the food and supplies they needed at the shelter. He would also occasionally help with the clients when the staff needed extra help. They had a hard time filling jobs at the shelter, because even though they paid fairly well, it was hard to find people who wanted to work at a homeless shelter. It was more of a calling than a job.

Not long after he started working at the shelter, he heard that Richard Harmon, the dump truck driver who had hit Elaine and the kids, had tried to commit suicide. Ed had struggled with his thoughts about the driver that had killed his family. At first he wanted to see him in prison. He talked to the prosecutor's office about what criminal charges could be brought. He had even talked to some lawyers about pursuing a civil case against him. Then the accident investigation was concluded, and the prosecutor's office had called and asked him to come down to discuss the results. They had gone over the maintenance records for the truck and found that the braking system had been rebuilt just a few weeks before the accident. They had also discovered that one of the new brake lines had been found to be paper thin due to something that had occurred during its manufacture.

The driver had literally been as much of a victim as Ed's family. If Ed wanted to pursue a lawsuit against the parts manufacturer, he would have a case. Ed thought about this and decided not to pursue it. He didn't think he could sit through the trial and maintain his sanity.

In the end he went to the Harmons home and tried to talk to Richard and let him know that he understood what had happened and didn't hold him responsible. It was one of the hardest things he had ever had to do. Richard Harmon was inconsolable. He said, "I can't sleep, can't work; every day and night is a nightmare." When Ed left, he knew that there wasn't anything he could say that would be of comfort.

He threw himself into the work at the shelter and tried to restart his life, but it just wasn't working. His moments of normalcy were brief, and he had to fight depression every day. He was on a treadmill; he worked as long as he could all day, went home to the apartment, killed time watching TV, and then he went to bed. Every day was the same, day after day.

CHAPTER

5

Laura Stevens went to college only because her parents insisted on it. She had never been away from home until she started her first year. She was a good student, but mainly because she just couldn't get into the social life. Her days consisted of going to class and doing her homework assignments. That was her daily schedule.

Then she met Travis. He was good-looking and charming, and he gave her a lot of attention. He was everything to her. When he asked her to marry him, she thought it was just what she wanted. Her parents tried to get her to wait until she finished school, but she wouldn't hear of it. At the end of her sophomore year they were married, and she quit school. He graduated and started to work. She stayed home and kept house.

But Travis was a party animal. After work he always stopped at his old haunts for drinks and to spend time with his buddies. After a while Laura figured out it wasn't just his buddies he was spending time with, so one night when he got home, she wasn't there and neither were her clothes. He didn't even try to call her parents' house to talk to her.

She filed for divorce, and when it was final she took back her maiden name and started looking for work. She didn't want to stay with her parents; she just felt like she needed to get away. She felt all at sea and needed to be on her own for a while so she could get her life together.

She sent out resumes to several companies away from her hometown. She got a reply from Merrill Industries in Granville and went in for an interview. When the interview was over, they told her that they had filled the job they had originally called her in for. But they offered her a job at the Merrill Homeless Shelter if she was interested. She wasn't sure about that, but she thought at least she would be away from home, and maybe she could keep her resume active at Merrill Industries and eventually get a job there. The idea of the shelter also appealed to her. She liked the idea that she would be helping people.

One of the first things she learned when she started to work was about Ed and his family. She couldn't imagine having to live through that. She was in charge of the housekeeping and food service area. This brought her into contact with Ed on an almost daily basis. At first their conversations were strictly related to business. After a few weeks she started to linger in his office for a while, and they talked about what was going on around the shelter.

Ed began to look forward to their conversations, and occasionally they went to lunch together. He didn't think of her in any romantic way; she was just an enjoyable person to talk to. He hadn't engaged in small talk with anyone since before the accident. Laura realized almost from the first that she felt something more for him than just friendship. Her feelings were different from anything she had ever had around a man before. She had never felt this way with Travis; Ed evoked a feeling in her that she hadn't experienced before. At first she wondered if it was just a sympathetic response to the tragedy he had experienced. She had shed tears when she first heard what had happened to his family. What she didn't realize—at least for a while—was that this was love. With Travis it had been physical attraction. Although Ed was a good-looking guy, she knew that wasn't the attraction. There was something else. There was a feeling even when she wasn't near him . . . as if she had left part of herself with him. She also knew that he wasn't responding to her the way she would have liked. It just wasn't the same with him. Only once when he had accidentally brushed up against her had she seen a flash of desire in his eyes. She had hoped that he was finally beginning to feel something for her. But it had never reoccurred. All she knew to do was to be patient and hope that eventually he would notice that she was interested in more than just a casual relationship.

This morning she was delivering a list of things needed for the coming month. She always looked forward to her visits to Ed's office, hoping that one day would be different. She hoped that she would detect some change, some indication that he felt something for her. He was always friendly but impersonal. Their occasional lunch never moved beyond friendly conversation, even though she tried to shift it to a more personal nature.

She had been divorced for about a year now, and she still felt a little stupid about letting herself get into such a marriage. She looked forward to coming to work just to be near Ed.

This morning he seemed a little distracted, so she put the paperwork in his in-box and left. He didn't even look up. She was a little concerned lately at how he seemed to be withdrawn and unresponsive to her presence, whereas he usually stopped whatever he was doing to enter into conversation. When she passed his office later he wasn't there, and when he hadn't returned by lunchtime she was a little concerned. It just wasn't like him to leave during the day for this long a time. She asked around the shelter, and no one seemed to know where he had gone.

CHAPTER

6

Ed sat looking at the list that Laura had just dropped on his desk. Looking at it, he just started to wonder what he was doing here. The whole place was depressing; it was a daily exposure to the human misery of transients, homeless, the drug-addicted, alcoholics, and schizophrenics. He thought, *I'm supposed to be helping all of these people, and I don't even know who they are. The problem is, they are on the streets, and if they don't report in to one of the shelters in the city, no one knows where they are. How do you help someone who doesn't even know they need help?* Some just disappeared and hopefully had found their way back into society.

It was a beautiful day, and he was feeling depressed and didn't want to deal with the problems at the shelter. He decided to chuck it all and go for a walk. Maybe he could get the latest news on what was happening on the street. The Sixth Street Bridge was a favorite hangout for some of the shelter clients, so he set off for the bridge. He hoped that Gabby would be there; he would know what was going on.

CHAPTER

7

Gabby had shown up a few months back and sort of took up residence under the bridge. He seemed out of place there because he was always neat and clean and well spoken. He didn't drink or use drugs and was very much a loner.

Not long after he arrived, some of the businesses along Sixth Street started noticing that the parking lots and streets around the area were always free of trash and the usual debris. Then some of them began to notice Gabby picking up things as he walked along the street and throwing them into the nearest trash can or dumpster. Some of the restaurants and fast-food places started giving him food when he came around, but he refused to take money. The supermarket manager asked him if he would take some food, and he said he could use some coffee. After that there was always a pot of coffee under the bridge for anyone who wanted it.

All the trash under the bridge and along the riverbanks began to disappear, and the river just seemed to be a cleaner, more beautiful, and more natural place. Ed had met Gabby several times, and he would always talk to him, but Gabby never started a conversation. He seemed to be well educated, and if you didn't know better, you would have thought he was a tradesman of some sort.

He also seemed to have an effect on those he came into contact with. Some of the homeless people who visited the bridge started to pick up after themselves and take more interest in their surroundings. Gabby seemed to have a positive effect on people. You couldn't be around him without leaving feeling better. Even Larry, the local bully, would not cross Gabby. There was never any confrontation, only a subtle submission to the wishes of Gabby.

CHAPTER

8

The bridge was a double-arched concrete structure about three hundred feet long over the Blue River. Most of the time the river wasn't more than a few feet across and maybe two or three feet deep, but in the rainy season it could turn into a raging torrent. Ed scrambled down the embankment, which was fairly steep and covered with weeds and boulders. On the far side of the first arch he could see Gabby, brewing his coffee. Ed jumped across the water and walked toward Gabby, who was tending to his fire and didn't see him coming. But as Ed neared him, Gabby looked back and smiled.

Then Ed glanced across the stream and froze in midstep. The arch on the other side of the water, starting at the base of the bridge and rising to the center of the arch, was covered with a mural of arresting beauty. At first it seemed to be a woodland scene, but there was something strange about it. Then he realized that it seemed to be too well ordered. The placement of everything in it seemed to be in just the right spot to enhance the overall beauty of the mural. Then he realized that it was more like a garden. Across the base was a stone wall about waist high, and on top of the wall was a wrought iron fence interrupted about every ten feet with a stonework post. In the center was a gated iron arbor. Inside the gate was an intricate paved stone pathway that wound away and disappeared behind the hedges and flowers on each side of the path. Ed walked back toward the garden, wading right through the water without even feeling himself getting wet. It seemed so real that you felt you could walk right into it. When he reached out to touch it, he expected to reach right into it and touch the flowers in the foreground. It was almost a surprise when his hand stopped on its surface. Then he noticed something else. It wasn't cold like the concrete abutment it covered. It was warm to the touch. He walked back across the water to the other side of the arch and turned to take in the entire scene. It rose from the base of the abutment to the center of the arch, where the sky slowly faded from blue to the color of the concrete. This wasn't a painting; you couldn't see a brushstroke in it. Then he realized that it was three-dimensional. It was like looking through a huge window at a scene of great natural beauty.

He looked at Gabby, who was now looking at him like he had just realized that someone else was there. Ed asked, "How long has this been here?"

Gabby hesitated and said, "Several weeks." That wasn't possible; everyone in the city would be talking about it by now if it had been here that long. Gabby handed Ed a cup of coffee. Ed took it without even realizing it. Then Gabby reached out and took hold of both his wrists. Ed started to pull back, but he couldn't move. He felt paralyzed. All he could see was Gabby's face and eyes. His mind went completely blank, but he could still see those eyes. They were filled with kindness, even love. Ed had no idea how long they stood there. It could have been seconds or hours. When Gabby let go of him and stepped back, he felt totally drained.

Gabby turned back to his fire, and Ed just stood there looking at the mural. It was hard to take your eyes off it. It was like studying a work of art, knowing there was a message in it from the artist and not quite being able to put your finger on the message. After he had studied it for a while, he realized he was holding the coffee and turned back to Gabby. Gabby stood there studying Ed with a smile on his face. Ed had completely forgotten why he had come down here. He looked back across at the mural. Without even thinking about what he was doing, he crossed back over the stream and walked up to the wall and reached out to touch it. It felt warm to the touch. He stepped back a few feet to try to take more of it in. He felt as if he were in a dream. He turned to ask Gabby about it, but he was gone. The fire was still there with the coffeepot sitting on a rock next to it. He heard a soft click and looked to see what had made the noise. It seemed to have come from the direction of the garden, but there was nothing there. He was still alone under the bridge and was at a loss as to what he should do. He was totally confused, and he thought that he would just wait for Gabby to come back so he could ask him about it. He started for the embankment while still looking at the mural, and then he froze.

My God, the gate into the garden was open. He thought, *I know that gate was closed; I have been looking at the mural ever since I got here.* He walked slowly to the center of the mural and stood in front of the gate looking into the garden. It almost seemed as if there was a gentle breeze blowing out of the garden carrying the scent of flowers. He reached out to touch the wall, and there was nothing solid there. He stepped forward almost involuntarily and stepped right into the garden. He felt a shiver run through him, and he felt as if he was floating on air; then he was suddenly very cold and then completely comfortable. As he stood there on the stone path, he heard a soft click behind him and turned to see the gate had closed. He stepped forward and came up against what he could only describe as an invisible barrier. He could see the underside of the bridge, and on the opposite side of the stream was Gabby walking under the bridge with an armload of sticks for his evening fire.

CHAPTER

9

He started to yell, but then Gabby looked over at him with a grin and a quick wave, and he returned to his task. Ed knew somehow that there was no going back until that gate opened. He felt compelled to follow the path. He turned and walked along the path, looking in wonder at the beauty of this place. The trees were perfectly shaped, and every plant seemed to be healthy. Every so often there was a small stone bench beautifully constructed and almost looking like part of the landscape. He felt totally at peace, as if a great weight had been lifted from him. It seemed like everything was growing at random, but at the same time it seemed to be laid out in some carefully constructed plan. The air seemed cleaner or fresher, and the temperature was perfectly comfortable. He felt like his senses were more acute, and his mind was perfectly clear. Every detail seemed to be permanently etched on his brain. He could smell the flowers and freshness in the air. After a while the pathway started to wind, and it climbed small hills and then descended into small valleys. It crossed over small streams on beautifully crafted small stone bridges. After a few minutes the trees and vegetation seemed to thin a little, and pretty soon he was walking through more open spaces and could see buildings in the distance.

They appeared to be farms. He could see silos and barns and outbuildings. Occasionally he passed another bench; they were like works of art made of intricately cut stone and beautiful wood. As he came over a little rise, he could see someone sitting on one of these benches.

Elaine watched Ed coming down the path toward her, and her thoughts flashed back to the first time they had met in the bookstore. From then on she had thought about him constantly. Everything from then on just seemed natural. She had moved in with him, and their lives became one. Now as she watched him coming up the path, she knew this would be just as natural to her. As she got up and started toward him, she knew just how this was going to feel. She had been at a loss as to how she was going to handle their meeting like this, but now she was relaxed and ready. As she got up and started toward him, he stopped.

He felt a little light-headed. He was at a complete loss; this was like some dream. He thought, *I would know that walk anywhere. It's Elaine.* She smiled as she came closer and then laughed. He felt as if he were losing his mind. Elaine was walking toward him, and while he knew it was her, there was something different about her. She looked younger. There was also an aura about her. It was more a feeling than something he could actually see. She was radiant. He stood there trying to respond to what could not be happening. When she got to him, she threw her arms around him and hugged and kissed him. He stood there holding her in his arms, completely unable to process what was happening. She took him by the hand and led him to the bench, and they sat there just looking at each other.

When Ed found his voice, he asked her, "Is this a dream? What is happening, and where are we?"

She looked at him and replied, "You are in The Garden. You have been allowed to enter it because there are things that you must do, and I have asked that I be the one to guide you and to let you know what they are."

Ed asked, "Am I dead?"

She laughed and said, "No, you may be more alive than you have ever been. You are, in effect, my guest for the next few days. Allowing someone from the outside into The Garden is very special. You should consider this a very special gift."

Ed asked, "Where are Michael and Teresa?"

She grew very quiet and then said, "I'm sorry, but they are not here; they have left The Garden. They were not old enough to stay. The experience of growing up and facing the challenges of the world outside is one of the requirements for staying here." She took Ed by the hand, and they continued along the path. His questions were coming almost too fast to ask. Elaine said, "I'll answer all of your questions, but you will have to be patient, because although most things here are the same as you're used to outside The Garden, some things are completely different."

They turned off the path onto a small paved walk, and there was a beautiful stone cottage at the far end. "This is my home," she said. "I had it built when I arrived here." It was beautiful and looked like it had been there forever. It seemed to be part of the landscape, and when they entered the cottage, Ed felt completely at home. He could see her personality everywhere; it was as much a feeling as any particular thing. There was a huge stone fireplace that went clear to the roofline. Across the room opposite the fireplace was a stairway to the upper floor. On the far end of the fireplace was the kitchen. The back wall was almost entirely glass. There was a veranda completely across the back of the house, and on one end it extended out to a gazebo. The view was spectacular. It overlooked a valley about a mile wide with a beautiful river flowing through it. He felt completely at home and then realized that he had felt that way when they moved into their first home. She had decorated and arranged everything then, and he hadn't found anything he would have changed. She made coffee as they talked, and then as they sat looking out the windows, she began to tell him about the accident and how it came about that she was here.

She had heard a horn honking loudly as she entered the intersection. She saw motion out of her left eye and turned her head just as the dump truck hit her. The last thing she saw was the driver's eyes and the horror on his face. Then it was like waking from a deep sleep and being confused about where you are. She became aware that she was standing next to the wreckage with the children, watching people run to the car to see if they could help. The car was unrecognizable. It was a four-door sedan crushed into a ball not much bigger than a small compact car. It was like seeing someone else's accident. She was just another bystander.

As she stood there, she heard her name called and looked toward the sound. There, where the bank should have been, was the most beautiful sight she had ever seen—a fenced garden, and standing next to a gate in the center of the garden was a man smiling and beckoning for her and the children to come to him. She would learn in time that his name was Gabby. He opened the gate, and somehow she knew that they had to enter. As she walked through the gate, she felt a shiver run through her. He took her by the hands and looked into her eyes. For a few seconds her entire being seemed to be suspended in time. When the feeling passed, she felt completely at peace. She looked behind her just as the gate closed. Gabby stood beside her smiling, and beyond him was the accident, surrounded by people. The first emergency vehicles were beginning to arrive.

She walked to a nearby bench and sat down with the children. She realized on some level where they were, but it wasn't at all the way she thought it would be. The children were quite calm and sat looking at the crowd on the other side of the fence. She thought, *I have to explain this to them, but what can I say? I don't understand this myself.* There was no sound coming from the crowd outside, even though she could see people shouting and the rescue squads working to get the doors of the car open.

She heard a soft voice call her name, and looking down the path going into the garden, she saw two people coming toward them. It was her grandparents, but they seemed much younger than when she had last seen them. They could have been her brother and sister. Her grandfather had died several years ago, and her grandmother not long after. This was incomprehensible. She sat there stunned, trying to figure out what was happening.

Her grandmother sat down beside her with tears in her eyes. She took Teresa into her lap and put her arms around her and smiled. "Elaine" she asked, "Do you understand what has happened?"

Elaine shook her head and said, "I'm either dreaming, or I am dead."

"You are dead," she replied, "but not in the sense that you have always thought death to be. You are in The Garden, and you will be here for quite some time."

"But, the children," Elaine said. "What can I tell them?"

Her grandmother said, "I know how you feel. They shouldn't be here; they are so young. They will be leaving The Garden soon because it is not their time yet to be able to stay."

"But I can't let them go," Elaine cried. "What would become of them?"

Her grandfather took her by the hand and said, "Come on home with us, and we will try to explain what is going to happen."

CHAPTER

10

When they had gone, Gabby reflected on what he had seen when he searched her soul. He knew that this was an unusually kind and caring person. In that brief few seconds he had seen a lifetime of kindness to and caring for others. He reflected on the highlights of what he had found in her. When she was still in grade school, she had found out that an elderly widow living alone on a farm down the road was having trouble fixing her meals. She told her mother about it, and they started fixing extra food and Elaine would take it to her. She would do little chores for her while she was there, just to make things easier for her.

When Elaine was in high school, her class went to New York City on a class trip. In her hotel room she dropped an earring, and while she was hunting for it she saw a billfold wedged between the bed and the wall. When she opened it, she was shocked to find it contained almost two thousand dollars. It also contained a foreign driver's license and a business card. At first she thought that she would turn it in at the hotel desk. Then she considered the amount of money, and she thought about the temptation the money would be to whomever she turned it in to.

The address on the business card was in Denmark. She got the long-distance operator and called the phone number. A lady answered in Danish, and Elaine started to apologize for not understanding. The lady instantly switched to English with a slight accent. When Elaine explained about the billfold, the lady grew silent and Elaine realized she was crying. Then she told Elaine that her husband had been to New York on business and had lost his billfold, but he didn't know where. Elaine asked her for an address where she could send it. She wrapped it and mailed it and knew she had made a good decision. A few weeks later after she had gotten home, she received a large package with a beautiful clock in it from Denmark. The note inside explained how much her honesty and kindness had been appreciated.

One day when she was driving home from the grocery, she saw a man with a white cane standing on the sidewalk, turning from side to side as if he didn't know which way to go. She stopped and found he was trying to find the bus stop. She walked him a few blocks to the bus stop, and he thanked her profusely.

Later, when she was in college, she was driving back to school after a weekend at home. It was late, and the weather had turned bad. It was pouring rain, and she was a few car-lengths behind the car ahead of her. She saw a truck coming toward them, and it met the car ahead of her just as they came to a narrow bridge over a drainage ditch. The car swerved to its right and left the road. It rolled over and slid down the embankment into the ditch, which was filled with fast-moving water. The truck didn't stop. Elaine stopped and put her flashers on, and she ran down the embankment. The windows on the front doors were broken out, and the car was damming up the water. It was flowing through the car and getting higher by the minute. Elaine ran to the downstream side and struggled to open the door. When it finally popped open, she got down on her hands and knees and looked in. There were four people in the car. They were hanging upside down on their seat belts. They were in a state of panic. She was on the driver's side, and the driver was a little disoriented. He said he wasn't hurt, so she told him to brace his arms against the roof; she was going to release his seat belt. She helped him get out, and then he helped his wife. Elaine opened the back door and helped two children out of the car. She loaded them all into her car and took them to the police station. Then she got back into her car and went home to change clothes and clean up, and then went on to school.

On a return from a trip to the West Coast with her mother to visit her aunt, she saw a serviceman on crutches trying to get a seat on the plane so he could get home. She went up to the desk and told the agent she would give him her seat. She spent twelve hours in the airport until she could get another flight. She didn't really think anything about what she had done. It was just the right thing to do.

After she was married, she was in the food court at a mall when she saw an elderly woman walking around seeming to be confused. She went up to her and asked if she could help. The woman was in the early stages of Alzheimer's disease, and she was lost and couldn't figure out where she was. Elaine sat down with her and talked to her for a while. The woman was carrying a handbag, and she let Elaine go through it. Elaine found a small address book and called the first number in it. It was the woman's son. She waited with the woman until her son arrived to take her home. It was such a small thing to do, but it was greatly appreciated by her son and her family.

Then there was the day that Elaine was getting ready to check out at the grocery. There was a young woman with two kids who were getting pretty restless. Elaine told her to go ahead of her through the checkout. When the cashier gave her the total for her groceries, she just slumped. She said, "I'm sorry, but I'm twenty dollars short. I'll have to put some things back." The cashier was a little put out, but Elaine just stepped up and handed the woman twenty dollars.

The woman asked her for her address so she could send her twenty dollars. Elaine just smiled and said, "No, this is my good deed for the day."

All these things were going through Gabby's mind while he stood there watching Elaine and her grandparents walk away. He knew that he was looking at a genuinely good person. He had read many souls that had shown up at the gate. Good people, but he knew this one was special and that he would be seeing her again. A lot of people did these things occasionally in their lives, but Elaine just seemed to be attracted to people in need.

Chapter

11

Elaine and her grandparents walked along the path for a while until they came to a beautiful farm. "This is our place," they said, "and you are going to stay here with us until you get your own place." She recognized the house and the barn and outbuildings. It looked just like their farm before it was auctioned after Grandmother died. They had tried to reproduce their old farm and at the same time make some of the improvements they had always wanted to make on the old place.

Her questions were coming so fast that she had to try to sort her thoughts and decide what to ask first. Grandma said, "Let's go into the kitchen and have a bite to eat." Although Elaine didn't feel at all hungry, Grandma set about fixing lunch for them. All the while she talked about how happy they were to see them again and how nice it would be to have the children around for a while.

Then Elaine remembered what Grandma had said earlier about the children not being able to stay. "Why won't they be able to stay here?" she asked.

"It wouldn't be fair to them, for one thing," her grandma answered. "They must experience growing up in an imperfect world. They will face challenges and experiences that would be unthinkable here. They have to know what life is like. They have to experience the happiness and sadness of life. They must learn the difference between good and bad . . . all of the things that people learn as they go through life. "All the people who live here are, for lack of a better term, 'mature adults.'"

Elaine felt sick. She couldn't bear the thought that Michael and Teresa would be taken from her. She knew she would never be able to reconcile herself to this. She refused to let them leave her. "I don't understand how anyone could ask me to do this," she said.

Her grandmother had tears in her eyes. She took Elaine in her arms and said, "Hear us out, honey. We will feel the pain of their leaving also. This isn't a decision that you can make. You will probably have several months before they have to leave. Consider this—no one is born into The Garden. You come here only after your death outside. That means that if the children were allowed to stay, they would never have children of their own. Their only experience from now to eternity would be a childless one. Could you take the experience of being parents away from them? You will have enough time to prepare them and yourself for their departure."

"Where will they go?" she asked.

Her grandfather answered, "Back," he said, "out of The Garden into a new life. They will be reborn and grow to adulthood."

Elaine cried and said, "No way will I let them be separated from me. There has to be another way."

Grandma took her hand and sat next to her, and she tried to explain, "They will not remember you, but they will know you when they return to The Garden.

"During the next few months you will be counseled, and Michael and Teresa will be prepared for that separation. While it will be painful for you, they will understand what is going to happen to them."

Elaine was heartbroken; the thought of losing the children like this was unbearable. It took several months of counseling by the group of mentors that were assigned to her and the children to prepare them for the eventual separation. In the end she realized the necessity of sending the children back, but it didn't make it any less painful.

The day finally arrived when Michael had to leave. Elaine and her grandparents, along with Michael and Teresa, accompanied their counselors along a path they had never taken before. It seemed to lead into a beautiful forest. After they had walked a short distance into the forest, they came to a small glade.

Elaine began to slowly discern the outline of some sort of structure. It seemed to be carved out of solid rock on the far side of the glade, with an entrance that at first looked like the entrance to a cave. The path led into the entrance. As they entered, it was like walking into a thick fog. Then they began to see light ahead. As the mist around them cleared, they could see a beautiful atrium. Elaine couldn't see where the light came from, but the very walls seemed to glow. In the center of the atrium was a small pool surrounded by plants. The path became circular and surrounded the pool, and then it continued to an opening at the back of the atrium. There were small semicircular benches around the pool. Their guides seated them on one of these benches.

Everything felt so comfortable. The very atmosphere was relaxed and inviting. A beautiful lady entered from an alcove on the opposite side of the pool and came to sit with them. Although Elaine had never seen her before, she thought of her as a family member. Although young-looking, she seemed to be ageless. She was at once motherly and grandmotherly. Her voice was soft and very reassuring. She talked to the children and held Michael in her arms. She seemed to be aiming the conversation at Teresa, but she was at the same time reassuring Elaine and her grandparents. After a few minutes she told everyone it was time. Elaine and her grandparents were in tears as they hugged Michael and told him good-bye. Teresa gave Michael a hug and kissed him on the cheek. While she understood what was happening, she didn't seem to be as sad as the adults. She understood that this was going to happen with her eventually, but she felt like she would see Michael again. The lady took Michael by the hand and they walked out of the back of the chamber and seemed to just fade into a mist.

Michael could remember walking through the mist, but from that point on it was like going to sleep and dreaming a happy dream.

CHAPTER

12

Madeline Purcell awoke with a sharp pain. She lay waiting for another. When it came, she nudged Roger. He rolled over, and she said, "I think it's time." They got up and got things ready and waited for the pains to get closer together. Roger called her doctor and told him they were headed for the hospital. A few hours later she delivered Troy.

Troy could never remember when the thoughts and dreams began. They were always vague. He remembered a beautiful blond lady and a tall man. Occasionally he could remember a small girl. As he grew older, they faded away. On rare occasions they might be a passing thought, but he never thought of them as real.

Roger and Madeline realized that at an early age Troy was fascinated with things mechanical. He paid little attention to toys that didn't move or make sounds. As he grew older, he was quick to learn how to replace batteries or put toys on a recharger. He loved Tinkertoys and Erector sets. He would spend hours building things. Then he would take them apart and build something else. He would be like this throughout his entire life.

CHAPTER

13

A few weeks after Michael left, it was Teresa's turn to leave. Elaine was still mourning over Michael's leaving, but she knew that she had to steel herself to the inevitability of what was going to occur. This time was different for Teresa. She was almost eager. She could remember the nice lady, and she was looking forward to seeing her again. It was hard to know if she realized that she would be parting from Elaine. She sat on Elaine's lap on the bench and watched for the lady to appear. When she came, it was the same as before. She just sort of materialized from the mist. She smiled and put Teresa on her lap. She talked to them for a few minutes and then had them say their good-byes. Teresa hugged Elaine and said, "Don't cry, Mommy. I'll be back." Elaine tried to smile through her tears. She kissed her good-bye and told her she would be waiting for her. Then they were gone.

Roy and Ethel Martin had been trying to conceive for a long time. They had almost given up when she finally got pregnant. They were happy beyond belief. When little Carolyn arrived, it was into as loving a family as she could have possibly wanted. The Martins were amazed at how quick little Carolyn was. She picked up on things very fast. She always seemed to be a step ahead of them.

When she reached school age, she was already reading and was pretty fast to pick up on math problems. She loved playing outside, and when Ethel worked on her flower beds, Carolyn was right there. She knew the names of all the plants and how to take care of them. As she grew up, she showed an interest in almost everything around her. She liked to be involved with anything going on around her. In the quiet moments when she was alone, she also had thoughts that puzzled her. She would find herself thinking about a beautiful lady who had been kind to her and the tall blond lady whom she sometimes dreamed of. As she grew up, they just seemed to be part of a childhood fantasy. Eventually, thoughts of them became more and more rare, until she had for all practical purposes forgotten them.

CHAPTER

14

Ed sat for a long time trying to absorb what Elaine had just told him. He wept at the thought of the children having to leave. He put his arms around her and held her. He knew how painful it must have been. He thought of his reaction when Elaine and the children had been taken from him. It was some moments before they both got control of themselves. Ed kissed her, and they sat silently with their thoughts for a while. "So, the children are back outside," he said. "Do you know where they are?"

Elaine hesitated and then explained, "Yes, they are with families that love them as much as we do." Ed thought about it for a few seconds and then realized that it might be better not to know where they lived. He could see himself constantly looking for them in every child he saw. He thought it better to drop the subject; he also felt like Elaine didn't want to go there.

Then he told her about Gabby and his experience before coming through the gate. "I don't know what happened," he said, "but it sounds like the same thing that happened to you."

Elaine took his hand and said, "I have talked to Gabby many times since getting here, and what you experienced was the reading of your soul. No one can come through the gate until the gatekeeper determines his or her worth. Everything you have ever heard, seen, smelled, said, experienced, or done . . . every thought you have ever had is recorded in your very soul. You may not be able to remember it all, but it is there.

"That is why you can have a memory of something pop into your head even though you were not even trying to remember it. Of all the organs in your body, the brain is the most important one because it controls the function of everything else. But it is your soul that houses your very being. Think about it. When you think about yourself, you don't think about your body or even what you look like. You think about that internal being that occupies your very soul. That is also why your soul resides there. You could become completely paralyzed and still know who you are. All the rest of your body functions to keep you alive, but your soul functions to tell you who you are. When you die, the entire body, including the brain, dies, but not that being that has occupied that body. What Gabby did under the bridge was read your soul. When he finished, he knew more about Ed Williams than Ed Williams does.

"He determined that you could enter The Garden. We refer to this place where we are as 'The Garden.'" Everything else is just the 'outside.' Make no mistake. Not everyone who walks through that gate will be on the same path that you took to get to me. There are many paths that lead to other places. The gatekeeper determines which path you will take. Some paths will lead to rebirth and return to the outside. I did not doubt that you would be allowed to enter, because I know who you are. Gabby and I have had many conversations about you. But only a gatekeeper could allow you to come here."

Ed asked, "How do they decide who enters and who doesn't? I have never been a particularly religious person. I'm afraid I never gave much thought to what would happen when I die."

Elaine was silent for a while. Then she said, "I haven't been here long enough to answer that, but I can tell you that it is more complex than how religious you are.

"I have had several conversations with Gabby, and he told me a story. There are two men. One man is friendly, outgoing, and generous. He is always the first to help out a friend in need. He is, however, an atheist. The second man, while attending church regularly, keeps to himself and pays little attention to the plight of others around him. He thinks of his religion in very personal terms. He seems to be incapable of relating his religious tenets to his relationships with others. Should the first man be refused entry to The Garden because of lack of belief? Or should he be allowed in so that he can ponder the fact of his existence after death? Should the second man be refused entry because he has been unable to understand the true meaning of his beliefs?"

Elaine got up and said, "I'll fix dinner while you think about all of this; then we can go out on the veranda and eat while we talk."

Wait," he said. "You still haven't told me why I am here. I don't understand why I have been allowed to come here."

She stopped and turned to him. There was a hint of tears in the corners of her eyes. Then she just took hold of his hands and said, "Be patient with me. I want you to get more acclimated to your surroundings here. I will explain everything to you when I think it is time.

"Would you like some wine with dinner?"

"Wine?" Ed asked. "You have wine here?"

She laughed again and said, "Things aren't that much different from what they are like outside The Garden. I could fix you a cocktail if that would be better."

Ed followed her back into the house and watched as she poured them each a glass of wine and then began to prepare dinner. "Where do the wine and food come from?" he asked.

"Everything is produced here just as it is on the outside," she said. "Tomorrow we will go to Grandpa's farm, and he can explain that to you better than I could.

"You never met my grandparents, did you? They were gone before we were married."

Ed and Elaine talked about their families and their life together as Elaine worked. Then they carried dinner out to the veranda.

Ed said, "Could you explain to me what happened with Michael and Teresa?"

She said, "During the first months while the house was being built and we were getting settled, there were two counselors who visited almost daily—one to prepare me for what was coming and one for the children. I was told that they would be going to people pretty much like us whose lives were pretty much the same as ours. While I would not physically meet these people, I would be allowed to know them, and if I didn't approve of them I would have other couples to study. But the children would not be able to stay longer than was necessary to match them with new parents."

Ed asked, "What do you mean, know them but not meet them?"

"I could visit the families that were eligible to receive them. They didn't know that I was there, of course, but I could feel their emotions and determine what their personalities were. I could determine what kind of people they were and how their children would be received. The children went to different families. Having them in the same family might have triggered memories of their previous life, and this could have caused them to be confused about what seemed to be inexplicable thoughts. They were only here for a few months. I can't tell you how difficult that parting was. It was like having to put them up for adoption. Only the thought that one day I would meet them again kept it from being unbearable. Since then I have come to realize that this is better for them and that I haven't really lost them. They are just away for a while. It has been the same with you. I knew that eventually we would be together again."

Ed was barely able to comprehend how difficult that had to have been. He knew Elaine was a strong person, but that had to have tested her very soul. He looked at her and said, "You know, I have noticed ever since I got here that while you are the same, there is also something different that I can't put my finger on."

She said, "Something happened to me after I got here. I can't really explain it, but after I had been here for about a year, Gabby took me into another Garden for a few days. I was assigned a mentor. When she had read my soul, she granted me the ability to spiritually move between The Garden and the outside. I still don't know why I was given this privilege. I understand that it is very rare. Then I was returned to The Garden."

Ed listened in awe. He couldn't rationalize what she was telling him. He felt, more than understood, the enormity of what this gift meant. She said, "In some ways you have been with me ever since. This is difficult to explain, but while I couldn't see you, I could feel your happiness or sadness, and unfortunately your depression, from that time on. To some extent I could know what your thoughts were. I have spent quite a bit of time crying for you because of the pain that you have felt. It's hard to explain, but I didn't know exactly what you were thinking; I only knew in a general sort of way. I probably know some things about you that you don't even know about yourself."

"Now I'm worried," he said, laughing. "I'll have to be more careful about what I think about."

"Too late," she said and laughed. Then in a serious tone she said, "I do the same with the children."

"Are they all right?" he asked.

"Yes, they are well loved and happy. They have no memory of their previous lives or us—at least none that they can recognize for what they are."

"I can't imagine how hard it must have been for you to watch them leave," he said.

"Think of it this way," she said. "If there hadn't been an accident, sooner or later they would have grown up and married. They would have led their own lives, and we would have lived on the periphery of those lives.

"We were told that we would know ahead of time when the time of conception would come. When that happened, their souls would simply pass into the ova at conception . . . first Michael, and then Teresa. I know they are happy, and to whatever extent I can, I will help them throughout their lives, even though it can be very little.

"Some children conceived in this way are more intelligent at birth. They don't remember their previous life, but some of them seem to advance mentally faster than other children. I can tell you that they are happy, but I won't tell you who they are. They are still young enough that they might be able to recognize you. They couldn't make the connection, but it could be a bit confusing. It has only been four years since the accident."

"Let's clean up the kitchen and sit out here and talk until bedtime." As she said that, she gave Ed that little smile that he hadn't seen for years.

"I hope you mean what I think you do," he replied.

"Come on, she said. "I'll wash and you dry." After the dishes were done, they sat and talked about memories and made small talk about their life together. They sat on a little wicker divan and snuggled a bit, and Ed could almost forget what had brought them to this spot.

As the sun hit the horizon, they walked back into the cottage and he held her in his arms and kissed her. She responded to the kiss, and all the old feelings flooded back, but oddly without the urgency that he used to feel. He almost thought he could feel her responses as well as his own. They walked up the stairs to her bedroom, and she showed him where the bathroom was and said he could shower while she turned down the bed. While he was showering, the door opened and she stepped into the shower with him and said, "I'll scrub your back, and you can return the favor." It brought back a lot of memories. When they crawled into bed, the feeling was indescribable. It had been so long, and now lying next to her flesh to flesh, he had the incredible feeling that she knew exactly what he was thinking and responded to his very thoughts. After a while he felt like he was responding to her thoughts as well.

They must have slept a little toward morning, and she woke him up at about sunrise and they made love again. Later, lying there in each other's arms, he knew that he would remember this night forever.

He dozed off and was awakened by the smell of coffee and breakfast being made downstairs. All the horror of the memories of the last time she had made breakfast for him came flooding back. He thought of the children and felt the emptiness in his life. It took an effort to pull himself together. He dressed and went down, and the table was almost set. They embraced, and she said, "I thought the same thing." There were tears in her eyes. It took him a second to realize that she knew what he had felt. Then she dried her eyes and gave him a hug and said, "The kids are okay. Let's eat. We have only four days together. We have to move on; we have a long day ahead of us."

Breakfast was on the veranda, and it occurred to him that the temperature was perfectly comfortable. So he asked her, "Is it always this nice?"

She said, "It varies from season to season, but the weather is never extreme in this area."

"So what if you like to ski or participate in winter sports?"

She said, "There are other areas in The Garden that are mountainous and have ideal skiing conditions. There are also some of the most beautiful beaches you could imagine."

"All right, so how do you pay for all this—your house, food, recreation, and everything else you need?"

"I work for it," she replied. "I'm not working now, because you are here, but when you leave, I will be back to work the next day. As I told you before, everyone here works. I think it may be one of the requirements for entering The Garden. Everyone I know does something to contribute. Some people have the same kinds of jobs they had outside The Garden, and others have entirely new vocations. That's because some jobs don't exist here. Everyone here works in some productive capacity. We have farmers, engineers, scientists, and educators . . . and, yes, laborers.

"When I need groceries, I just go to the store and get what I need and walk out."

"Whoa," I said. "There is no exchange of money or credit?"

"No, it's basically a system of barter; you work and receive no pay, so you receive what you need and you don't pay.

"We live by natural law—basically, the laws of God. It would never work on the outside, because mortals are involved, and they are always going to twist the system to their own benefit. Here we know with certainty that we answer to a higher power."

"Think about where we are," she said. "There are no laws except the ones that you feel in your heart. You know what is right. Your word is your bond. There are no contracts; your word is good enough. When you are outside The Garden, no matter how strong your faith in a supreme being, there is always this little doubt in the back of your mind. Don't you agree? Once you enter The Garden, you know. You know! We all answer for ourselves.

"Here there is no cruelty . . . no crime, meanness, jealousy, or pettiness. That is all left behind. Here all we feel is love and happiness. We don't have policemen or a military. There is no need. Besides, once you are here, you suddenly understand the simplicity of it all. You can travel anywhere you choose and never have to worry about your safety or whether you have enough money, or about getting lost. I choose to live in a cottage in the country because it is the kind of life I'm comfortable with. If I wanted to, I could live in a mansion or a beach house. I work; we all work."

"What do you do?" he asked.

"I work on my grandfather's farm; we are going over there after breakfast. The nice thing about it is you get to pick your job, and I could work just about anywhere I wanted to. I grew up on my dad's farm, and Grandpa needs the help, so for now that is what I like to do. Okay, enough talk. Let's clean up here and head for Grandpa's."

CHAPTER

15

Laura was concerned. Ed had left before lunch and hadn't come back. He never did that, and she had this feeling that he wasn't coming back today. He had been very withdrawn for the last few days, and nothing she could say or do seemed to help. She asked Gary Hunt the shelter director if he had seen Ed and he said no. When he hadn't returned by quitting time, she went to his apartment to see if he was ill. She had a key that Ed had given her some time back so she could check on things while he was traveling to seminars. There wasn't any answer to her knock, and she thought about going in but changed her mind, thinking he might just be shopping or something, so she left.

As she walked toward her apartment, she saw Gabby coming toward her and thought maybe he had seen Ed. When he got to her, she started to ask him, but before she could get it out he said, "Ed isn't going to be back for a few days, and he wants you to check on his apartment for him." She asked where he was, and Gabby said, "He is taking a few days off for personal business." He seemed to be a little evasive about it, but she didn't know what to say. Why had Ed told Gabby and no one at work? She wouldn't have accepted this from anyone else. But she always felt reassured when she was in Gabby's presence. He just made you feel comfortable. He was like a trusted old friend even though she had known him for only a short time. He said Ed would be back on Monday and that he wanted her to tell his boss that he would see him then. This was Wednesday, and she couldn't imagine his taking five days off work without saying something.

She knew he had been acting a little depressed and hoped he was just trying to work things out. When Gabby left, she returned to Ed's apartment and went in to check on things. Everything was as neat as a pin. She wandered through the apartment for a few minutes before she realized that she really didn't want to leave it. She told herself to get herself together; she was acting like a love-struck teenager. The problem was that she was in love. She decided to leave and come back tomorrow to check on the apartment again. She knew it would be all right, but she just liked being there. It was almost painful for her to think about walking into Ed's office knowing that he didn't feel the same toward her.

CHAPTER

16

After getting everything in order, Ed and Elaine walked up the path to Elaine's grandparents' farm. When they got to the farm, the path started to parallel a road. The road looked to be concrete and was in perfect condition. "Where does the road lead?" Ed asked.

She said, "It goes to the village and then to the manufacturing and processing plants for the crops produced here.

"We have a superb rail passenger service from the villages to the cities and anywhere else you choose to go. Most transportation here is by rail. Trucks deliver everything locally. Some people have cars, but you really don't need one. We have what we call autocab. I can request a cab, and it will be sitting at the end of the path when I tell it to be there. It is fully automated and will take me wherever I tell it in the village, and I can tell it when and where I need it to take me back home."

The farm looked like a picture. Everything was carefully tended and neat. She stopped walking and gave Ed a sly little look. "Okay," he said, "what do you have up your sleeve? I still know what that look means."

She laughed and asked, "Do you remember Curly?"

"You mean as in The Three Stooges?" he said.

"No," she said, "as in Curly, your dog when you were a kid."

"How in the world do you know about Curly? I have never talked about him to you," he said.

"Well, he lives here," she said.

Ed teared up. The last time he saw Curly was when the vet was putting him to sleep. They were best buddies when he was a kid; he had him from a puppy until he was twelve years old. He was just a mutt, but they were practically inseparable. "He was about forty pounds with a reddish curly coat, and he seemed to understand everything I said. My parents had prepared me for the time when he would die, and I had understood. But when the time came, I couldn't believe the anguish I felt as he drew his last breath. I never had another dog. It was just too painful.

"I had tried to shut him out of my mind, and I had been pretty successful until now," he said.

Elaine gave him a hug and said, "Let's go. He is waiting for you." As they were walking up the path to the house, the door opened and Curly came roaring out to meet them. He could barely contain himself, and Ed wasn't far behind. Ed got down on his knees and hugged Curly and thought he would lick his skin off. Elaine was crying, and her grandparents were crying when they got to the door. Curly wouldn't move three feet from him the whole time he was in The Garden.

He had never met Elaine's grandparents; they had died before he met her. Elaine introduced him to Albert and Edna, and they walked into the house. They didn't look like they were as old as Ed, and they didn't act like it either. While he didn't know them, they seemed to know him. Elaine explained that when she and the children arrived in The Garden, they had lived with Albert and Edna while she got settled and the cottage was being built.

They had gotten Curly from Ed's great-grandparents the day before he got here, and he would go back to them when Ed left and live with them until he returned. "How did you know I was coming?" Ed asked.

They just looked at Elaine and said, "We knew."

They visited for a while and toured the farm while they talked. Ed had more questions than he could ask. Then Elaine said, "Tomorrow we will visit your great-grandparents on your father's side; they have been waiting also, but we thought one family at a time might be better. We realize how overwhelming this can be."

"My great-grandparents? I've never met them; I don't know anything about them," he said.

"Well, they don't know you either," she said, "but they know of you. Family means a lot here, and when new people arrive, everyone in their family is interested in them and their lives. Friends are also aware when someone new arrives, so new arrivals can expect to get a lot of attention and support when they get here. Because you are a visitor, your visitations will be pretty much members of our immediate family." Ed began to get a suspicion that there was something he hadn't been told yet and she was waiting for the right time to tell him.

The men sat on the patio while Elaine and her grandma made lunch, and Ed talked to Albert about his farm. He said it operated pretty much the same is it did on the outside.

"How many acres do you farm, Albert?"

"About one thousand," he replied. He was a dairy farmer, milking about two hundred head. He also raised grain, mostly corn, soybeans, and hay. The milk was picked up every morning and delivered to the dairy to be processed. He hauled the grain to an elevator, and it was transported by rail to wherever it was needed.

"You can't do that by yourself, can you?" Ed asked.

He said, "No, Edna and Elaine put in some pretty long days. Occasionally if we need help with something, a neighbor will help out. Most of our neighbors are relatives, and we share in the work when it gets to be more than you can handle by yourself."

"But you don't get paid for it?" Ed asked.

"No, there isn't any exchange of money, if that's what you mean. I farm because that is what I like to do, and anything I need I get in exchange. Just look around; what more could someone who has lived on a farm his entire life want? I get all the pleasure and rewards of farming and none of the headaches. There are no mortgages, crop insurance, and worries about diseases or crop failures. The weather here is perfect most of the time. It is a perfect life for a farmer."

Ed said, "It is also a lot of heavy work."

Albert said, "Yes, but that is one of the things that I enjoy doing, and here you never get older and you don't have any of the pain or crippling injuries that you get on the outside."

"What about injuries?" Ed asked. "Surely you can get seriously injured, even here."

"Yes," he said, "you can, but every injury heals itself. Even if you lose an entire limb, it will regrow almost overnight. Look at Elaine—you know how badly mangled she and the children were in that accident. When their souls entered The Garden, they had to be reborn. They looked the same, but they were more like images of themselves than actual physical bodies. Within hours they transformed into a physical form. Everyone comes into the Garden whole, both physically and mentally, no matter what his or her affliction. When you walked through the gate, you became physically and mentally pure.

"Because you are a visitor, when you leave, your aging process will start again, but past physical problems or injuries will be less noticeable."

After lunch Elaine, Curly, and Ed went for a walk. They talked about their life and how happy they had been. He told her about his life after she was gone, skipping over some of the lowest points.

She interrupted him and said, "I know what you have gone through, because I have followed you through the whole experience. For me it was like having someone tell me what was going on more than actually seeing or experiencing it."

She stopped Ed now, and looking him straight in the eyes, she said, "You are going to have to move on. The last few years you have been leading half an existence. You are a young man, and you can't go on this way for another fifty or sixty years. You have the opportunity to make a difference not only in your life, but in many lives. That is why you were allowed to come through that gate. I have presented your case, and I expect you to not let me down."

Ed felt as low as he had ever felt in his life, because he knew she was right. He cried, and she took him in her arms and held him until he had pulled himself together. He felt that she had more to say but was saving it for later. They walked on, and she pointed out some of the beauty that unfolded around them. Occasionally in the distance you could see a house or barn.

They finally returned to the path that led to the farm, and he said, "What about Curly? What happens to him when I leave?"

"Don't ask me how, but he knows that you are going to leave. But until you do, just try to get rid of him—he has stuck to you like glue since he first saw you."

When they got back to the house, they sat on the patio with Albert and Edna and talked about their lives and what kind of adjustments it took when they were finally both in The Garden. Edna said it wasn't much of an adjustment for her; a much younger-looking Albert had met her at the gate and explained where they were. When they reached the farm, it was just like coming home from a long vacation. She realized that she looked younger too. All the pain and weakness were gone. The feelings of well-being and serenity were palpable. Elaine said that was her experience as well.

Ed told them that he noticed some changes in himself, but he thought maybe they were all in his mind. It could just have been the peace and serenity of this place and the fact that all of his problems were outside where he couldn't do anything about them anyway. They said they thought those feelings were probably accurate, but he probably really was feeling better physically because while he was here he would get physically a little younger.

Later Edna and Elaine fixed potatoes and salads while Albert grilled steaks and he and Ed talked. After dinner they wandered around the barn and outbuildings. Albert was very proud of the equipment that he had accumulated in the time he had built up his farm. His milk parlor was completely automated, and he said they were constantly updating it as the technology improved. He explained that everything was in top mechanical condition. Every year the manufacturer sent out technicians to go over everything and bring it into like-new condition. Ed was surprised to see that the equipment had the names of the manufacturers on everything, and it was the same as you would see on the outside. Albert asked him why he was surprised. All of those people that have come to The Garden just took up where they left off on the outside. Every inventor and manufacturer ever born was here if they had made it into The Garden.

That brought up another question. "What happens if you don't get into The Garden?"

Albert paused and then said, "There are gates other than the one we all used to come into The Garden. There are people that you will never see again. It is pretty tough on their loved ones, but you grieve and go on. There are also gates within The Garden that lead to other Gardens. This is not the end of our journey; it is a waypoint."

Ed had to think about that for a few minutes. He said, "I'm afraid I don't understand. If this is a waypoint, then what is the destination?"

Albert laughed and said, "If anyone knows that, I would love to hear it. You know, there are people here who have been here for thousands of years. Then there are some who won't be here for more than a few hundred. Occasionally, maybe once or so a month, there is a ceremony when some people leave this Garden to move to the next. Anyone can go to the ceremony, but it is mostly relatives and friends. It's a time to say good-bye and celebrate their passing on to the next Garden. Some of those people have been here for hundreds or thousands of years. They have reached a level of understanding that can be had only through many years of living and studying here. This is sort of a cosmic classroom, and when you are ready, you move on."

Ed said, "You have my head spinning. I am going to have to digest that for a while."

Albert stopped and said, "You may as well hear this from me, and I should tell you not to say anything to Elaine about what I am going to tell you. It makes her feel embarrassed. Elaine is very special here. She was called home in that accident. She is highly respected and consults with the gatekeepers about things . . . just like bringing you here. There are often people who wish to bring people here who need help. She talked to the gatekeepers about bringing you here, and they did a lot of investigating before they allowed you in. She is allowed to pass into and out of The Garden—not physically, you understand, but she has been watching you for years now. She knew that you were in trouble. That is why you are here. She will bring it up in her own good time. So be patient and let her decide when to talk to you about why you are here."

They walked back to the house and joined the girls on the patio, and they all talked until the sun started to set. Then Elaine and Ed walked back to the cottage with Curly following along. They talked for a while on the veranda and then went up to bed. Making love this time was much less urgent and much more tactile. It was like old times when they were still experimenting and discovering each other's bodies. Later they lay there just enjoying the contact and the nearness of each other. Finally, Ed asked, "Why can I be here for only four days?"

Elaine was silent for a while before she said, "Experience has taught us that beyond four days, readjustment to the outside becomes very difficult. You may not realize how much stress and physical and mental discomfort you shed when you walked into The Garden, because you just unconsciously began to feel better. But when you walk back out, it will come back in an instant. You will see more clearly the coarseness and incivility. Some people have barely been able to cope with the burden that they instantly assume.

"That is also the reason why you will meet so few people while you're here. There are many members of your family here that you don't even realize you are related to. Most were here long before you were born. Now, it is time for you to go to sleep. Tomorrow is another busy day."

CHAPTER

17

Waking up in The Garden was a new experience every day. Ed felt like a new person every morning. Breakfast this morning was on the veranda again, and it was an incredible experience to sit here without a worry in the world and just enjoy life.

After breakfast they headed to his great-grandparents' place. They lived in town, and Ed and Elaine walked to the end of the path, and there sat an autocab. "How did this get here just when we needed it?" Ed asked.

"I called it," she replied.

"Explain that; you don't have a phone as far as I know," Ed said.

"That is a little hard to explain. It's sort of like mental telepathy. I just think it, and it shows up."

Ed just shook his head, and as they walked up to the cab, the door opened and they got in and sat down.

It was about the size of a small sedan with four seats. Ed and Elaine sat in the front, and Curly jumped in the back and acted as if he knew exactly where they were going. As soon as they were seated, the autocab took off for town.

In a few minutes they started to see a few houses and small buildings, and pretty soon they were in the town. It was fairly small, and Elaine said about five thousand people lived here.

They turned into a side street with a cul-de-sac at the end. The lot sizes seemed to be about two to three acres, and the houses, though all different, appeared to have been built by the same builder. Everything was beautifully landscaped. The homes almost seemed to be a part of the landscape. They pulled into a driveway, and two people were waiting for them.

As soon as Curly jumped out, he was wagging his tail and watching to see if Ed was staying. As soon as they were all out of the autocab, it left.

This was another really strange experience. Ed had never seen these people before except in some old photos that he hadn't really paid much attention to. Now they were young-looking like Elaine's grandparents. He had to search his memory for their names. He thought they were Frank and Alice, but he wasn't sure. Elaine came to his rescue, saying, "Hello, Frank. How are you doing, Alice?"

Alice gave Ed a big hug, and there were tears in her eyes. She looked at him and said, "I don't quite know how to explain how I feel meeting a great-grandson I've never seen before. I can see your father in you when he was your age."

Frank just stepped in and said, "It is good to meet you, Ed. We have been eager to meet you ever since we heard you were coming."

They took them around to their patio, and everyone sat and talked about the family. Frank and Alice asked about Ed's grandparents. Ed's grandfather was their son. Ed said, "My grandparents are in their seventies and seem to be getting along pretty well."

Frank said, "We are hoping that when they come into The Garden, they will settle here close to us. We were a pretty close family when we were on the outside."

Ed had to admit that he hadn't seen much of his grandparents lately. After the accident he had pretty much cut himself off from the rest of the family and everyone else. He promised himself that when he got back he would go to see them and spend more time with them. His perspective had changed enormously in the last three days. He was beginning to see his life in ways that he had never even thought about before, especially regarding people and his relationships with them. For the rest of his life he would know about The Garden and how his life would be perceived by the family members who lived here.

Frank worked for the transportation system, which wasn't much different from his job on the outside, where he had worked for a railroad. That brought up a question that had been puzzling Ed for the last couple of days. "If The Garden has a railroad, then how big is it compared to, say, the United States?" Frank grinned and then floored him with his answer.

"The Garden is infinite. People have been coming here for ages, and you still have plenty of open space for farming and development. There are cities that are as populous as any on the outside, but it is because the people living there like the big-city life. We live here because it is what we are comfortable with. We can also have a place on a beach or in the mountains—anywhere we would like to spend some time—and still have this place here."

"So, how much leisure time do you have?" Ed asked.

"Pretty much whatever we like," he said. "But I probably work more here than I did on the outside. We have the ultimate in what you would call flextime. If you really enjoy what you do, it really doesn't seem like work, don't you think?"

"I guess that is true," Ed said, "but after a while I could see it getting a bit old."

"That is true," Frank replied, "but anytime you like, you can change jobs and try something else.

"Think about this. Imagine living in a twenty-year-old's body with the wisdom of a two-hundred-year-old . . . or, for that matter, a two-thousand-year-old. While you're at it, try to imagine having perfect recall—being able to retain everything you have ever learned. Outside The Garden, by the time you have accumulated enough knowledge to be of any use, you are getting too old to make use of what you know." Ed had to stop and think about that for a while. It was a little mind-boggling.

Another question occurred to him. He asked, "If I could walk through the gate from the outside into The Garden, where exactly *is* The Garden? The gate I walked through was on a concrete wall with a dirt abutment behind it."

Frank sat for a moment trying to find the right words. "I'm not sure I can answer that. The way I think of it is that it's like a parallel world. When you go back to the outside, remember that we are in some ways only an arm's length away. The boundary between us is like a window, and the only time that window opens is when you die or, in some instances such as yours, it is opened for you."

"So who decides when a living person can come through the gate?" Ed asked.

Frank glanced at Elaine and said, "That's easy. It's the gatekeepers. They are the only ones who can open the gates."

"But," Ed replied, "I didn't see a gatekeeper when I came in."

Elaine laughed and said, "Are you sure?"

Ed thought about it for a second, and then it came to him. "You mean Gabby?"

"Yes, Gabby. He has been watching you for longer than you know.

"He talked to me several times about you, and he agreed with me that it would be beneficial to a lot of people if you could come in for a visit."

"But Gabby has been around town only for a month or so," Ed said.

She said, "No, he has been there for centuries, but, like The Garden under the bridge, you couldn't see him until he decided to reveal his presence.

"Listen, from the first spark of conception to the last breath we take, we are followed through life by the specter of death. From our first gasp for breath to our last, it is by our side so close we could reach out and touch it. We are totally unaware of its presence until times of extreme danger or serious illness, but it is always there. Only when we reach that last gasp do we realize that it wasn't death at all. It was the gatekeeper of life. It opened the gate that let our soul into the world, and it will open the gate to let it into The Garden. It wasn't an enemy but a friendly escort that knew us better than we knew ourselves."

This answered a lot of questions Ed had had about Gabby. "You said 'gatekeepers' earlier. How many are there?"

Frank answered, "I'm not sure any of us knows, but there are more gatekeepers than almost any other group of people here. You entered under a bridge; Elaine entered on the side of a bank. Some people enter from hospitals or nursing homes, or even their own homes. The gate can open anywhere there is a need. When you saw The Garden, it wasn't happenstance. Gabby knew you would be coming before you did. Your arrival was planned. In short, you were summoned to that bridge."

"But why?" Ed asked. "Why me? I can't begin to imagine why I would be brought here."

"Before you leave here tomorrow, it will be clearer to you," he replied. "Elaine will tell you what you must do."

"One more question, Frank. Everyone refers to this place as 'The Garden.' Is this The Garden of Eden?"

Frank sat in silence for a moment, and tears welled up in his eyes. Then he said, "No, you are going back to the Garden of Eden—a despoiled garden ruined by the human race. People like you are the only hope to ever restore it to any semblance of what it was meant to be."

Ed said, "If it is up to me, we might be in a lot of trouble."

Frank looked at him and said, "You don't have to carry that burden; you just need to do whatever you can to improve your part of it."

They had lunch on the patio and talked about family and what it would be like when they all met again. Frank said, "It can get a little confusing sometimes. We have become good friends with family members that we had never even heard of until we got here. A family reunion here would draw thousands of people. We do have small get-togethers occasionally, but usually only two or three generations . . . and that can be in the hundreds."

Alice interrupted saying, "Frank, you're going to talk the poor boy to death. Ed, you and Elaine are staying for dinner, so you have plenty of time to talk this over. Frank, you can come and help me get things ready for dinner while Ed and Elaine sit here and just relax for a while. We will fix something to drink and snack on until dinner is ready."

When they had left, Ed looked at Elaine and said, "Okay, what is it you are going to tell me about when I leave The Garden?"

"It will have to wait until we get home," she replied. She seemed a little saddened as she said it.

When Frank and Alice came back out, they talked mostly about what was going on outside The Garden. They asked questions about people and families that were still there, and Ed tried to answer with whatever he knew, which wasn't much. "I'm afraid I haven't been overly social since the accident," he said. "My life was turned upside down, and I'm afraid I haven't handled it too well." They were very understanding, but he could detect a reluctance to express everything that they were thinking. Elaine was quiet during this discussion, and he felt she was weighing her thoughts about what they were going to discuss later.

After dinner they stayed for a while, until Elaine finally said it was time to be going. After a few tearful hugs the autocab had returned, and they walked out and got in, with Curly close behind. "Shouldn't he stay here?" Ed asked.

"No," Elaine said. "He might as will stay with us until you have to leave." The ride home was pretty quiet as they both sat there in thought about tomorrow.

When they got to Elaine's, they sat by the fireplace in silence and dreaded tomorrow coming. Elaine seemed to be better prepared than Ed for these last few hours together. Finally she turned to him, and he thought she was going to tear up, but she composed herself and took his hand and said, "I am going to say some things that you may find strange, but they need to be said.

"For starters, tomorrow you are going to have to change the way you have been living. I should say *existing* because you have been stumbling through life insulating yourself from the world around you. You have people who care for you, and they haven't been able to get through the wall you have erected around yourself. You are surrounded by people who need what you can do to help them. I know you, Ed; I know what you're capable of and what kind of person you are. I know you better than anybody does. You haven't let yourself feel anything toward the people who love you most.

"Gabby has told me that you have a friend, Laura, that you occasionally have lunch with. How do you feel about her? Have you ever asked her out? How does she feel about you?"

Ed sat silent for a few seconds. Then he said, "I don't know how I feel about her. As you said, she is just a friend. I like being around her, but we are just friends."

Elaine looked at him and took a deep breath. "You are hiding from your true feelings. She is very much in love with you. Don't you know that?"

"How can you say that? I have never so much as held her hand," he said.

"Trust me," she said. "I am well aware of how she feels. I also know that you are in love with her, even if you haven't figured it out yet. The trouble is, you have feelings of guilt because you think that to love her would be unfaithful to me."

"But I still love you. How could I love her and not feel unfaithful to you?" he said.

She teared up and said, "Look, I still love you too, but we are living in two different worlds. You may live another forty or fifty years. You have to live your life, not isolate yourself from it. Look me in the eye. It is hard for me to say this, but I am telling you it is all right to love someone else, and Laura is that someone. Trust me about this. I know it to be true."

Now Ed teared up. "I'm not sure how to feel about this," he said.

She said, "Just remember that I will still be here when you next walk through that gate, and if Laura comes through it first, I will be waiting for her too."

Then Ed asked her, "Have you found someone here that you love?"

"No," she said, "and I haven't looked, but it is possible, and if I should find someone, I want to know if you could accept that."

"I don't know if I can answer that; I will have to think about it," he said.

"Well," she said, "while you're thinking about it, I may as well bring up what else we have to talk about.

"You have just been going through the motions since the children and I were killed. There are a lot of people who need your attention, and you have just been doing enough to get by, both personally and professionally. I know you and what you're capable of, and you haven't been giving it. I can't tell you what you have to do when you go back, but you will know, and I can tell you that I and others will be watching and helping all we can. Tomorrow is going to be the start of a new phase of your life, and it is going to be better than it has been for the last few years while you moped through your own personal hell. I want you to give all you are capable of, and know that I will be rooting for you in everything that you do. I know you well enough to know that you won't let me down. You are returning to an imperfect world, and no one expects you to be able to change it. But you can change your part of it for the better. That's all that can be expected of anyone. From time to time you are going to be faced with problems that you won't know how to handle. When that happens, I will be there to help. Sometimes you may know that I helped, and other times you won't; but know this—you will never be alone."

He knew that everything she was saying was true and felt both embarrassed and ashamed. "I understand," he said. "And listen, if you find someone here, you have my blessing. One thing I know is that we will always have our love for each other." They went out onto the patio and watched the sunset, and, reluctant to end the day, they stayed there in each other's arms long after dark. When they went up to bed, it was with the realizations that tomorrow they would part for what could be a very long time and that the next time they met things would be very different. Making love was bittersweet, as they both knew this would probably be the last time.

Sometime later Ed awoke. Wondering what had awakened him, he realized Elaine wasn't there, so he got up and dressed and went downstairs. She was sitting in front of the fireplace, and at first he thought she was asleep. She had an aura about her that almost glowed. He felt that she was not quite real, but when he got close she looked around and smiled a sad smile and motioned for him to sit down beside her. "I couldn't sleep," she said. "I think I'll stay up the rest of the night and watch the fire. How about some coffee?"

"Sounds good to me," he said, and he went in to the kitchen with her to watch her and just to be nearby.

She looked at him and said, "I was with the children when you came down."

"You mean you were thinking about them?" he asked.

"No," she said, "I was with them. I could hear their soft breathing as they slept. I do that often; it reassures me that they are all right, and somehow my presence comforts them. I have been doing the same thing for you, but it hasn't worked so well, has it?"

"I don't know how to answer that, but I feel bad that I didn't know," he said.

"How could you?" she said. "Who would believe what was happening to them? I'm sure you felt something; you just didn't know what it was."

"Can everyone here visit their family like that?" Ed asked.

"No," she replied. "I know I was given that ability by my mentor, but I don't know why. There are some others who can visit the outside, but it is very rare. I also am in a unique position to be able to change a large number of lives through you. I want you to think about this. We are all about family here. We are very aware of our ancestry, since we see our ancestors frequently. When you get back outside, just remember that. It is easy to get involved with everyday life and forget that it is all about family."

We drank coffee and talked until sunrise. He helped her fix breakfast, and they sat and talked and tried to prepare themselves for the parting, which was only a few hours away now. She said, "I have something that I want you to do; this is important to me, and I want you to do it as soon as you can when you leave The Garden."

"Consider it done," he said, "anything you want if it's humanly possible." Then she explained what she wanted done, and Ed smiled and said, "It will be done by the day after tomorrow."

She said, "I know I don't have to tell you this, but I have to say it anyway. You have to be very careful about whom you tell about The Garden. To start with, most people will think you have gone off the deep end, but you will know whom you can trust with the knowledge." She stood up and looking at him said, "It's time to go." He thought she was going to say something else, but she just smiled. They started down the path with Curly in tow, and Ed tried to take in everything he could so that he could remember all of this for the rest of his life.

CHAPTER

18

Laura Stevens decided it was time to break for lunch, and as she walked out of the building, she saw Gabby standing by the curb. Gabby smiled and said, "I've been waiting for you."

"What's up?" she said. She had seen Gabby practically every day since Ed had left, and they had developed a friendship. There was something comforting about talking to Gabby. It was hard for her to realize that he was living under the bridge.

He said, "I have something you have to see down at the bridge."

"Will it take long?" she said. "I have to get back to work right after lunch."

"Not too long," he said. "But you won't want to miss this." He helped her scramble down the embankment to the river, and she turned to look under the bridge. She had been down here before when they had had a drive to clean up the riverbank a few months back.

She stood frozen looking at the mural on the underside of the bridge. When she could speak, she asked, "How long has this been here?"

Gabby chuckled and said, "For quite a while." She walked along the riverbank looking at the garden and marveling at the beauty of it all. In the center of what she could only think of as a beautiful mural that stretched across the entire width of the bridge, there was a gate. Gabby walked up to the gate and, to her amazement, walked right into the garden. He turned around and held out a hand and said, "Come on. There is someone here you will want to see." She stopped dead in her tracks. This was just impossible; it couldn't happen. She looked at Gabby, and he smiled and said, "It's all right. Come on in, and I will explain everything to you."

Then he did a strange thing. He took her hands, and all she could remember after that was his eyes. She didn't even remember stepping through the gate, but she heard a soft click and turned to see the gate had closed behind her. She turned back to Gabby, and he took her by the hand and led her to a bench a few feet inside the gate, and they sat down. Once he had explained where they were and why she was here, she was sure she was going to wake up at any moment and find herself at home in her bed. Then he said, "Come on. We need to walk a little farther in, where we can sit and wait."

Ed and Elaine were just coming over a small hill when he saw a couple of people sitting on a bench by the path. As they came closer, he realized who they were; he looked at Elaine, who was smiling that gotcha smile.

"What's going on here?" he asked.

"We all have something to talk about," Elaine replied. Gabby and Laura stood as they neared, and Laura looked questioningly at Ed.

Then Gabby stepped forward and said, "Laura, this is Elaine."

Laura sat back down. "I think I feel a little faint," she said.

Elaine sat down by her and said, "I don't blame you. This has to be quite a shock."

Laura asked, "What is happening to me? This is impossible."

Elaine stood up and asked, "Do you think you could take a little walk with me?"

Laura stood and took a couple of steps. "Yes," she said. "I'm all right now; I just can't take this all in."

Elaine looked at Ed and Gabby and said, "We are going for a little walk. You can wait for us here; we shouldn't be too long."

After they were gone, Ed sat down and looked at Gabby. "Maybe we should have a little talk ourselves," he said.

When Elaine and Laura came to the next bench, Elaine took Laura's hand and said, "Let's sit here for a while and talk." She looked at Laura and asked, "Do you love Ed?"

Laura was quiet for several seconds, and then she blushed and said, "Yes, I do . . . very much, but he doesn't love me. I don't know how to talk to you about this. It is a little embarrassing since you are his wife."

Elaine with tears in her eyes took Laura's hand and said, "I will always love him, but he is very alone. I cannot be his wife. We are separated by death. You are mistaken if you don't think he loves you. I have felt his love for you for some time now. The trouble has been that he felt guilty about loving someone else. As crazy as it sounds, he felt that to show his love for you would be unfaithful to me. We have discussed this, and I told him that he has to get on with his life. Our life together is over, and wishing it weren't doesn't make it so."

Laura cried and put her arms around Elaine. "I can see why he loves you so. I think I love you myself. I promise that I will love him as deeply as you do, and I will always remember this time we have had together."

Elaine gave her a hug and said, "Take my hands." They sat facing each other, and Elaine held both of Laura's hands and looked into her eyes. Laura felt mesmerized. She couldn't move. Then images began flashing through her head. At first they were pictures of people in miserable conditions, and as they flashed by they slowly began to look familiar and seemed to be less miserable. Then they began to look happier, and finally they seemed to be completely at ease. Laura couldn't identify any of these people, but they seemed to be familiar. Then she slowly became aware of Elaine looking at her and realized they were no longer holding hands.

Tears were running from Laura's eyes. Elaine put an arm around her and said, "I needed to have you see this. When you return to the outside, you are going to find some of what you saw. You are going to know that you can help these people. You will find a great peace and satisfaction in your ability to help others. Now let's get back; it is time for you two to go. Don't be surprised if he starts showing you a whole new Ed when you have left The Garden."

The girls were gone for a long time, and when they came back over the hill, they were laughing and talking like the best of friends. Ed just looked at Gabby and shrugged. "This is a little out my depth," he said. They stood as the girls came up, and Elaine hugged Ed and they kissed good-bye. Then Elaine turned and hugged Laura, and a little misty-eyed she said, "Take good care of him; you won't find many like him."

Laura was already teary-eyed and said, "Thank you for this," and she gave her a hug. Then she turned and took Ed by the hand and said, "I think I'm late getting back from lunch." They both laughed, and with a last wave and good-bye they turned and walked back to the gate. It opened as they approached it, and when they had stepped through it, they heard that soft click. When they looked back, they were looking at a concrete wall covered with graffiti.

They just stood there in each other's arms for a while, and then Ed said, "I owe you an apology."

"For what?" she said.

"For being a total fool," he said. "Let's go tell Gary you're taking the rest of the day off. We have a lot to discuss."

They spent the afternoon sitting on the riverbank talking about the last few days, and he told her about The Garden. "What did you and Elaine talk about?" he asked. "You were gone for quite a while."

"Girl talk," she said. "Someday I might tell you about it, but not until I know you a lot better."

He laughed and said, "I'll hold you to that." They talked about where they were going from here, and he said, "Let's start from now. I have quite an adjustment to make in my life, and I need to put all of this into perspective. I hope you are a patient person. So, what are you doing for dinner tonight?"

She looked him in the eye and said, "I'm dining with the person I love."

She gave him a kiss, and he returned it and said, "I'll pick you up at six." They parted and went home to change clothes and mentally prepare for the reality of their new lives.

As the gate closed, Elaine turned to Gabby with tears on her cheeks and said, "We have to talk." Gabby took her by the hand, and they walked to the bench and sat. She looked at him and said, "I would like for you to look out for him. He is going to need a lot of help with the burden I have given him. Will you help me?"

Gabby laughed. "It's a little outside my job description, but don't you worry. He won't even know I'm there."

Elaine gave him a hug and said, "I will need your help too. My ability to persuade people outside The Garden is pretty limited."

Gabby just smiled and said, "I'll be in communication with you whenever you need me."

She stood and gave Gabby a hug and a wave and headed for home.

When she got to the house and walked in, she realized how empty it was going to be. She had been living alone since the children left and hadn't felt lonely. Now that Ed had been there, it felt twice its size and totally empty. She thought about Ed and Laura, and the tears came. She knew she was being foolish, but she had just sent her husband to be with another woman. Then she started to think about the task ahead, and she started to smile.

With Gabby keeping an eye on things, the two of them should be able to help Ed and Laura without their even knowing it. Curly ran up to her and whined. She rubbed his head and said, "I know. I miss him already too. I guess it's time to take you home."

CHAPTER

19

The next morning Ed headed for Richard Harmon's. He was the dump truck driver who had killed Elaine and the children. He was living in a dumpy little house in a run-down neighborhood. He worked at menial jobs for short periods of time and then went off on an alcoholic binge until he was completely out of money. His wife, Ruth worked in the supermarket and pretty much kept them going. That she stayed with him was a testament to her love and character. She knew what was driving him, and no amount of talk would bring him out of it.

When Ed knocked on the door, she was just getting ready to leave for work. When she saw who it was, she wasn't sure what to expect, but Ed smiled and said, "I need to see Richard."

She hesitated and then turned and said, "Richard, someone is here to see you."

When he came to the door and saw who it was, Richard said, "I don't want to talk to you. Nothing you have to say can change anything."

Ed just stepped into the living room and said, "Let's see. If what I have to tell you doesn't change anything, all you have to lose is a few minutes' time."

Richard hesitated and then said, "All right, come on in." Then he told his wife, "It's okay go on to work." When she had left, the two men sat down, and Richard looked like he could cry.

Ed braced himself and said, "You are not going to believe what I am about to tell you, but hear me out, and then I will prove to you that what I am about to say is the absolute truth. The only thing I ask of you is that you not tell anyone what I am about to tell you.

"I can't tell you everything about what I have experienced in the last few days, but I have talked to my wife." Richard looked at Ed with what could only be described as alarm. Ed said, "I don't blame you for what you're thinking. I'm a bit incredulous myself. I told you I would prove to you what I am about to say. Elaine told me to come to you and tell you something that would prove what I have to say. Only you and she know what I am about to say. The last thing she ever saw on this earth was the look of horror on your face just before the collision. She said that you and she were looking each other right in the eye."

Richard broke down, the tears rolling down his cheeks. He said, "I dread falling asleep. I see her eyes and the startled look on her face every day and night. If I concentrate on something long enough, I can keep that horrible sight away. But at unguarded moments I see her face, and I can't bear it."

Ed got up and put a hand on Richard's shoulder. He said, "She told me to tell you that she understands you were not at fault. She is happy where she is, but she feels genuine anguish when she thinks about how you have let this destroy your life. There is nothing she would like better than for you to get yourself together and lead a happy and prosperous life. My greatest fear is that you won't believe this, because I promised her I would come to you and tell you this, even if you thought I was totally insane."

Richard sat there quietly for a while, and then he looked at Ed and said, "I believe you. The reason I believe you is that lately I have had some dreams where I could see her, and she would tell me almost exactly what you just said. I thought it was just a subconscious attempt to excuse myself for what happened that day."

Then Ed said, "Look, I would appreciate it if you didn't repeat this to anyone, not even your wife, unless you think she will understand it. If you need help to get things back on track, feel free to come to me, and I will do whatever I can to help."

It was a different person who walked Ed to the door, and Ed knew Richard was about to turn his life around.

CHAPTER

20

The next day Laura moved in with Ed, and the week after that they were married. After the honeymoon they started looking for a house and began talking about having a family. They found a small house a few blocks from the shelter and bought it. It needed a little cleaning up, but it was within walking distance to the shelter, and they both liked it. Ed thought about selling his old car but decided they would need it when they visited their parents.

When they got back to work, Ed went at his job with a vengeance. He hadn't even noticed how dreary the shelter looked; everything had been dreary for him. He went to Gary and asked if they could redecorate the rooms and put fresh paint on everything. Gary said, "I'll talk to John Merrill and see if they will give us the money."

Ed said, "Tell him all we need are the materials; we will do all the work ourselves."

Gary looked surprised. "That is a lot of work. Are you sure we can do it ourselves?"

Ed said, "I think so. We may have to get a few volunteers, but we will get it done."

When he talked to Laura about the project and told her they were going to do the work themselves, and hopefully get some people to volunteer time, she said, "Let me take care of that."

"What do you have in mind?" he asked.

She just said, "Let me know when you need help, and I'll see what I can come up with."

Even Ed was surprised at the number of people who showed up to help. Laura had got on the phone and contacted every church and fraternal organization in town. She contacted Merrill Industries, and Merrill employees signed up to volunteer in droves. Pretty soon they had to start scheduling people so everyone wouldn't show up at the same time. There were Merrill retirees and some contractors who came in with equipment and even materials. In a few weekends they had brightened the whole place up.

Ed began spending every spare minute visiting the haunts of the homeless people around the shelter, and he convinced as many as he could to come in and spend their nights. For some time now an idea had kept going through Ed's mind, and he couldn't let it drop. Merrill Industries owned about six acres around the shelter. The Merrill Shelter was on the southeast corner, and on the north side of the property was a three-story brick building that had once been a warehouse. It had sat empty for several years and they had talked about tearing it down, but for some reason they never got around to it. The shelter was always pretty busy, but it was getting close to capacity, and the warehouse was sitting empty.

Ed went to Gary and asked him why they couldn't remodel the old warehouse and expand the shelter into it. Gary was all for it, but he didn't think Merrill would give them the money it would take to get any of the warehouse space livable. "Look," Ed said. "That place is an eyesore the way it is, and we both know that some of our own clients sleep in it from time to time. All we need is permission and maybe money for materials, and we can turn it into a dormitory."

Gary said, "I'll talk to John Merrill about it, but I can't make any promises." A couple of days later John Merrill visited the shelter, and he, Ed, and Gary walked out and looked through the warehouse. John had several questions about what they had in mind.

Ed had most of the answers. "First," he said, "we have to be sure the structure is sound. It seems to be weatherproof, so we would like to divide the first floor into rooms and maybe even a couple of apartments for homeless families."

John interrupted. "I had the building inspected about three years ago with the idea of using it for office space, and it passed the inspection. I would have to check to see if the zoning needs to be changed.

"Let's do this. You need to talk to someone who can lay out a floor plan and see what needs to be done about wiring and plumbing."

Gary said, "I have a friend who works for an architectural firm. Let me see if he will look at it and give me an estimate of what it will take."

Two weeks later, they had a plan. Ed couldn't believe what they had come up with. The architects did their layouts and estimates for nothing. They seemed to be enthusiastic about what they were trying to do. The zoning commission gave them a thumbs-up and said they would send out notices; if they didn't have any complaints, it would be all right to start with their plans.

John Merrill was on board, but he said the costs were going to be a bit hard to meet. He could cover most of it, but they were going to have to figure out what they could do without. Laura had been excited about the project from the beginning, and she and Ed had talked about it at length while the plans were being formed. As she and Ed and Gary were talking about what they would have to cut out, she said, "Look, before we start to cut anything out, let me see what I can do to get some help from some of the people who came forward to help with the shelter remodeling." A few days later she walked into Ed's office and said, "Let's go talk to Gary." Ed knew she had something going by the way she looked at him. When they all got together, she said, "I don't think we're going to have to cut anything. In fact, we may not have to spend as much as we originally thought. I have several people who are willing to donate materials and labor. Give me copies of your floor plan, and I will let them see exactly what we need."

Within a month the first few rooms were ready for paint, and the flooring was ready to be laid. There were some families at the shelter that were ready to move into the apartments, but there wasn't any furniture. Laura went back on the phone. In an hour she said she had just talked to a furniture warehouse that would sell them enough furniture for the new facility at cost. The money they had saved through using volunteers would cover the cost, and they would still be under budget. The one thing that they hadn't discussed in all their planning was the exterior of the building. It was brick, and though it seemed structurally sound, it looked pretty bad.

Ed said, "Look, we can rent a pressure washer, and I will work on it on weekends." He went to a tool rental store a few blocks away and asked the owner, Dan Harper, about pressure washers. "What do you want to wash?" he asked. Ed explained what he wanted to do, and Dan showed him the washer he needed and explained how it worked. "Do you have a truck to haul it in?" he asked.

"No, but I will get one," Ed replied.

"Never mind. I'll bring it by after work."

When Ed walked out of the shelter that evening, there was a pressure washer and a scaffold that would allow him to wash all three stories of the building. It took him a couple of weeks to pressure-wash the dormitory and the shelter, but when he had finished, they looked like completely different buildings.

He called Dan and told him he was finished and asked him if he could come and pick up the washer and the scaffolding. Dan was there in half an hour and loaded up all the equipment. Ed asked him how much he owed him, and he said nothing. It was something he had wanted to do for a long time. Any improvement in the appearance of those buildings would help the property values in the neighborhood. Ed thanked him profusely, and as he left he started to think about all the contributions that had been made and all the volunteers who had come forward in the last few weeks. He recalled what Elaine had told him—at times she would help him, and sometimes he would know she had helped, and at other times he would not realize that she had helped.

The next morning when he woke up, he thought about the things Elaine had told him and realized that some of the things that had happened in the last few months must have been as a result of her intervention. He lay there and wondered if he really tried, if he could feel her presence. He knew she wasn't there. He rolled over, and Laura was looking at him and asked what was wrong. He explained what was going through his mind and asked her what she thought about it. She hesitated and then said, "I have had several dreams—or what you might call visitations—with her in the last few weeks. She is definitely involved in what is happening to us. She also told me to congratulate you."

"For what?" he asked.

"For being a father again," she said.

He couldn't begin to describe his feelings. "Did you know?" he asked.

"No," she said. "But I knew as soon as she said it, that it was true."

"Don't you think you should see a doctor?" he asked.

"Not yet," she said. "Let's give it another month."

"Why didn't you tell me?" he asked.

"Look, I don't know for sure. All I have is the word of Elaine, who has been dead for . . . what . . . five years?"

"I see your point," he said. "But in view of what we know about her, I think you can be sure that you are pregnant."

CHAPTER

21

An idea had been percolating in Ed's head for months, and now he was sure he wanted to press ahead with it. When he presented the idea to Gary, all he got was a look of incredulity. "That would cost a fortune," he said. "And what good would it do?"

"Okay," Ed replied, "but would you ask John Merrill for his permission if it doesn't cost him anything?"

Gary thought it over and said, "I have a meeting with him this afternoon and I'll see what he says, but I won't push the idea, because I don't see the necessity."

Later that afternoon Gary walked into Ed's office and said, "I don't believe it. John didn't even hesitate; he just said he wanted to see what you have in mind before you start." Ed spent the evening in the public library looking through lawn and garden books for pictures of stone walls. When he was just about to give up, in the last book in his stack he turned a page and there it was. It wasn't perfect, but it was as close as he could imagine finding. It was a how-to book for building stonework and stone paving.

He checked out the book and took it home to show Laura. She looked at the picture and at Ed and said, "You aren't serious."

"Serious as a heart attack," he said.

She shook her head and asked, "What can I do to help?"

"I'm not sure where to start," he said. "But I'm going down to the stone quarries and talk to them to see what I need and how much it will cost." The next day he showed the book to John, and after a few seconds' hesitation John said, "It looks like a pretty big undertaking, but go ahead."

Ed drove down to the quarry that afternoon. He showed the office manager what he was going to build and explained what it was for. He said he needed any help he could get because he had never tackled anything like this before. The office manager's name was Rick, and he said, "Let me get someone in here who has done something like this before."

He called someone out in the yard, and a big burly guy came up to the office and was introduced as Jerry. Rick explained to Jerry what Ed wanted, and Jerry looked at the picture and scanned through the directions and said, "It's pretty accurate." Then he said, "You know, this is going to take several tons of stone. It will all have to be cut to size and dressed before you can even begin to lay it. Have you ever done this before?"

Ed had to admit he hadn't. Jerry looked at Rick and said, "How much do you think it would cost for the stone?".

Rick sat down and started to calculate and came up with some figures. Ed's heart sank. All he could say was "Thanks for your time, but I don't think I can come up with that kind of money."

"How many feet of wall are we talking about?" Rick asked.

Ed said, "I haven't measured it, but I would guess about two thousand feet."

Rick laughed and said, "You're talking about a small fortune just for the materials, and you would have to have some work done with a backhoe and probably a mixer for the mortar. If you haven't done this before, I'm afraid you're looking at an impossible job."

Ed agreed and thanked them for their time.

"Listen," Rick said. "Give me your phone number, and if I can come up with anything that might help, I'll give you a call."

Ed left and drove back to the shelter pretty depressed. When he got there, Laura was in his office. "You got a call," she said. "Somebody named Rick, and he left his number."

Ed called him right away. Rick said, "Jerry and I were talking after you left, and he reminded me we have tons of scrap left over from when we cut stone for contractors. It would be one hell of a job cutting it and getting it usable, but if you want to try it, Jerry said he would bring up a load and dump it and you can try your hand at it. If it works out, we will give you all the stone you can handle."

"Great," said Ed. "Bring a load, and I'll see what I can do."

The next day Jerry pulled up in a dump truck and dropped a pile of stone behind the shelter. After work Ed and Laura went out and looked at it, and at each other. Laura shook her head and said, "I think maybe we bit off more than we can chew." Ed agreed. On Saturday Ed went to the hardware store and bought some of the tools listed in the book as being necessary to build a stone wall. The problem was the book didn't tell you how to cut the stone or what the dimensions were. It also didn't tell you what to use to cut the stone into the sizes you needed.

As Ed stood there pondering where to start, someone said, "Whatcha doin'?" Ed turned, and there was Larry. Larry was a big guy who came into the shelter when the weather turned bad and lived down along the river when it was nice. His reputation was that he was a bully, and most of the people in the shelter just gave him a wide berth.

Ed said, "I'm going to build a stone wall from here to the warehouse and enclose the entire compound."

Larry looked around at the buildings and back to the pile of stone. "You ever done anything like this before?"

"No," confessed Ed. "This is going to be a learning experience."

Larry was silent for a moment, and then he said, "You're going about it all wrong."

Ed looked at him and asked, "Do you know how to do this kind of work?"

"Yep," said Larry. "I've built stone walls before."

"Where?" asked Ed, surprised.

Larry shuffled his feet a little and then said, "I dropped out of high school and went to work for a stonemason. I worked for him for three years. You need some power tools. For starters, you need a stone saw. All these pieces of stone have to be cut to size. Let's see what kind of wall you're thinking about." Ed showed him the picture.

Larry looked it over and then said, "I've seen a wall like this before. I'm not sure you can do it. But if you want, I'll help."

Ed couldn't hide his surprise. "I wish you would," he said. "I was beginning to think it was impossible. If we're going to work together, maybe I should know your name."

Larry offered his hand and said, "It's Larry Ellison"

Ed said, "Let me go down to the tool rental store and see about getting a saw."

When he walked into the store, Dan Harper looked up and said, "What kind of trouble am I in now?"

Ed said, "I need to rent a saw to cut stone. Do you have anything like that?"

"Sure," said Dan. "How much stone are you going to cut?"

"Several tons," he said.

Dan did a double take. Then he said, "What are you building?" When Ed told him, he said, "You are talking about a pretty big project. How long do you expect it to take?"

"I really don't have any idea, but we will cut the load of stone we have and then start to lay it. If everything goes all right, we'll order more stone and start cutting again. I don't know how long it will take."

"Okay," Dan said. "I'll let you use the saw, no charge. But you will have to pay for the saw blades."

"Great. When can we get the saw?"

Dan said, "I'll have one of the boys bring it right down, and I will come down and show you how to use it."

When they unloaded the saw, Dan showed Ed and Larry how to use it. Larry said, "I've run one before, but it wasn't quite like this." The saw was water-cooled, so they had to hook it up to a hose and run an extension cord to it. In a few minutes Larry was measuring and cutting stones like a kid with a new toy.

Dan looked around and said, "How are you going to dig the footings for the wall?"

Ed looked a little uncomfortable and said, "I hadn't got that far yet."

Dan said, "Let me make a phone call, and maybe I can get someone to dig it for you."

Ed said, "I hate for you to have to go to all this trouble."

Dan just laughed and said, "It's no trouble, and it will improve the neighborhood."

On Monday morning a guy showed up with a backhoe and dug a trench for the footings in a couple of hours. The next day Ed got a phone call from a cement company with the news that they would sell him the concrete for his footings at cost. When he walked out of the office that afternoon, there were people in the trench putting in the forms for the concrete. "Who are these people?" he asked Larry, who was supervising the installation.

"Damned if I know," he said. "They just showed up and started unloading lumber. One guy set up a transit, and they went to work."

Once the concrete was poured, it was just up to Ed and Larry. They got a mixer for the mortar from Dan, and the next morning there was a pallet of mortar and a pile of sand sitting behind the shelter. They had no idea where it had come from. Larry showed Ed how to mix the mortar, and they started laying stone.

From then on, no matter when they started to work, people showed up and started to help. Some were clients of the shelter, and some just walked in off the street. A few had some experience, and others did whatever they were told, and soon they were able to jump in and fill whatever job was needed. Ed had never done anything he enjoyed more than watching the wall rise stone by stone. When the first ten-foot section was finished, Ed stood back in amazement. It looked remarkably like the wall around The Garden.

He looked at Larry and said, "Have you seen a wall like this before?"

Larry looked a little sheepish and said, "Yeah, I've seen one somewhere." Every day when Ed showed up to work on the wall, Larry was already at work. He would look up and say, "Hi, boss."

Ed would laugh and say, "No, you're the boss. I'm the hod carrier." They worked every evening and all day on Saturday and half a day on Sundays. Larry worked on it every day. He seemed to thrive on the work.

One Monday morning Laura walked into Ed's office and handed him a bill for concrete. He looked at it and gulped. "I didn't realize it would be this much." He looked at her and said, "I have to pay for this myself."

"No, you don't," she said. "We have to pay for this ourselves."

He gave her a hug and said, "I've got the money, but it's going to put a dent in my account."

"*Our* account," she corrected.

He laughed and said, "I stand corrected." When they had finished the stonework, he was almost sorry. It had been a labor of love, and it was beautiful.

Now, he thought, *how am I going to get the wrought iron for the top and for the gates?* It would have to wait for a while, but eventually he would finish it. A week later as he was walking to work, he could see someone working behind the building next to the wall. As he walked closer, he couldn't believe it. There was a crew installing wrought iron on top of the wall, and they were unloading gates and arbors. He walked up to a guy who was directing the work and asked, "Who ordered all of this fencing?"

He said, "It beats me. I just got a work order to install this ironwork."

Ed went into the shelter and tried to find someone who knew where the fencing had come from, but everyone was as surprised as he was. Ed walked out into the walled area between the shelter and the warehouse.

It looked pretty barren. Some trash, some old barrels, and other odds and ends had been thrown there over the years. As he stood there planning what he would have to do, he heard the familiar "Hi, boss." There was Larry, looking over his handiwork.

Ed said, "It looks like there is still a lot of work to do here, doesn't it?"

"Yeah, it does," Larry said. "Listen, boss. Leave this up to me."

"What are you going to do with it?" Ed asked in surprise.

Larry just said, "I'll take care of it." True to his word, in a couple of days everything was gone. Larry came into the office and asked, "What now, boss?"

Ed looked at him and asked, "Are you tired of laying stone yet?"

Larry said, "It felt real good, boss, getting back to doing something useful. What do you have in mind?" Ed pulled a couple of sheets of paper out of his desk and showed him what he was thinking. Larry looked over the papers and said, "I'll start on it tomorrow, but we may need some more stone, and a plumber."

In the center of the garden (they were now referring to it as the garden), they built a small pond with a fountain, surrounded by a stone path. Starting at the back door of the shelter, there would be a winding stone path that went to the fountain and then from the other side of the fountain to the dormitory. There would be pathways leading off of the main path that led to small grassy areas. In these areas there would be picnic tables and benches.

CHAPTER

22

Laura woke Ed up at about midnight with the news that she was having labor pains. They got up and started timing the pains. They decided it was time to go to the hospital, and a couple of hours later, she delivered. When the doctor came out of the delivery room, he said, "Congratulations. You have a daughter."

When Ed got to Laura's room, she said, "What are we are we going to name her?"

"What did you have in mind?" he asked. They had talked about several names but had never been able to decide.

"How about Elizabeth?" she said. "We will call her Liz."

"Liz," he said. "It sounds good to me." He went home and called in to say he would be taking off a few days. He and Laura had to decide what they needed to do about work.

When Laura and Liz got home from the hospital, the grandparents got there almost as soon as they did. It was a hectic few days, but the grandmas took care of everything. It was decided that one of the grandmothers would stay for a week, and then they would switch for the next week. They would keep that up until Laura decided she could handle everything. By the second week Laura had taken charge, and it was time for the grandmas to go home.

When Ed got back to work, he had a lot of work to catch up on. At the end of the day as he was getting ready to leave, he met Larry in the hallway. "Come on," Larry said. "I've got something to show you." They walked out the door into the garden, and it was amazing. Someone had planted trees and shrubs and laid out flower beds. There was sod in the grassy areas. "Who is doing this?" Ed asked.

"Everybody," said Larry. "People just show up with plants and trees, and everyone starts working.

"A lot of your clients are even doing some of this. Some friend of Dan's at the tool rental store showed up with a landscape plan and told us what kinds of plants and trees should go in the areas along the pathways . . . and then it all just came together."

Ed felt humbled. He couldn't believe this was even possible. Then he realized how much he had underestimated his fellow man. He couldn't wait to get home and get Laura and the baby so he could bring them back to see it. He just told Laura to get the baby and get in the car because he had something she had to see. When they walked through the gate into the garden, she was stunned. They both just stood there and took it all in. He explained how it had all happened, and she just hugged him and said, "You realize, don't you, that you are the one who did this?"

"No," he said. "I had the idea, but people pitched in here that I didn't even know. I have no idea what inspired them to do it."

"Yes, you do," she said. "Just think about it."

He looked at her and said, "Elaine?"

Laura nodded and said, "I see her hand in all of this."

The next day as he walked into the garden, he saw someone sitting on a bench. It was John Merrill. John looked at him and said, "I never dreamed it would be so beautiful and so peaceful."

"Neither did I," Ed answered.

They sat and talked for some time, and Ed realized that this man who was the president of Merrill Industries was as common as the janitors who worked for him. They conversed easily like two old friends. They talked of family and mutual acquaintances. Later Ed noticed that John walked through the garden almost daily. For himself Ed walked through it every day, and he often sat on one of the benches and thought about problems he was looking for solutions to. It was uncanny how often he solved the problems while in the garden.

A few weeks later he was in the garden when John sat down on the bench beside him. After talking for a while, he said that he had offered a job to Gary at Merrill Industries. He wanted Ed to take over for Gary at the shelter. Ed accepted immediately. John asked whether Laura had decided what she was going to do about her job. Ed said they were pretty much at an impasse, because she would like to continue working but didn't know what she would do about Liz. Then John asked Ed if he knew that Merrill Industries had a day-care center at the plant. It was the first Ed had heard of it. John said, "Why don't you and Laura drop by and look it over? If you like it, you can use the day-care center; a lot of our employees do."

Ed was relieved; he and Laura had been wrestling with this problem for weeks. After he and Laura had visited the center, they found it to be the answer to their problem. Laura started back to work, and every morning Ed would drop Liz off. They could drop in anytime during the day to check on her, and they could pick her up in the afternoon.

Ed was in his office when he looked up and saw Larry standing in the doorway looking a little unsure of himself. Ed said, "Come on in, Larry. What's going on?"

Larry came in and sat down and said, "I've got a job, boss."

Ed said, "Great. What are you going to be doing?"

Larry said, "You remember that landscaping guy that laid out the garden? Well, he asked me who did the stonework on the wall, and when I told him I did, he offered me a job. I've found me a little apartment, and he said he would give me an advance on my salary so I could move in right away. I just wanted you to know and to thank you for getting me headed in the right direction."

Ed sat for a minute and then said, "I would like to ask you something. You don't have to answer if you don't want to. You had a reputation for being a bully around here when you first showed up. What happened?"

Larry smiled. "I met Gabby," he said. "He straightened me out."

Ed got up and shook his hand and said, "Good luck with the new job. If you ever need anything, you call me. You know, I'll never forget the days we spent building the wall."

Larry nodded and said, "The same to you. Anytime I can help you, let me know."

Laura became Ed's right arm at the shelter. She was a natural at solving problems and understanding the problems of clients coming into the shelter. Laura seemed to have an almost uncanny ability to connect with people. In just a few minutes people seemed to be at ease with her. She seemed to be a natural counselor. She often walked in the garden with clients and talked to them about their problems. Many a person walked out of the garden with her, a better person.

A year and a half later Eli was born. They had kept in contact with Elaine's parents, and they visited often. They had practically adopted Laura, and when Eli was born they couldn't have been happier that they had what they considered another grandchild.

At the shelter the garden had begun to mature. The trees were getting taller, and the flowers and shrubs were filling out. Ed had been aware for some time that the garden was taking on a presence of its own. People in the surrounding area drifted into the garden just to sit and talk and relax. The clients of the shelter spent time in the garden almost daily. Gradually they had continued to remodel the dormitory, and it was filled almost to capacity. Laura had even started reading classes for the illiterates in the shelter. This led to basic classes on how to present yourself when applying for jobs. She also set up a program to bring in Alcoholics Anonymous and a referral program with the local mental health clinic. The effects of these programs were immediate and dramatic. The number of people coming through the shelter and progressing into useful employment was dramatic.

CHAPTER

23

One afternoon as Ed was sitting in the garden John Merrill sat down with him for one of their usual chats. Then seemingly out of the blue, he asked Ed if he would like to come to work for Merrill Industries. Ed hesitated and then asked, "Doing what?"

John said, "We would like for you to run our accounting department."

Ed was speechless. Finally he said, "I would love it, but whom are you going to get to run the shelter?"

"Whom would you recommend?" John asked.

There was only one person that Ed knew could do that without missing a beat. "Laura," he said.

John said, "That would be my choice as well. Take a week to get things arranged, and then report to me at the plant."

Ed walked into Laura's office and said, "Let's go for a walk." She could tell from the way he said it that something was up. They walked out to their favorite bench in a far corner of the garden and sat down. Ed said, "How would you like to run the shelter?"

Laura looked at Ed in shock. "Are you serious?" she asked.

"Yes," he said. "And John agrees that you are the right person for the job. What do you think?"

She said, "I think I would love it."

"Well," he said, "you've got the job."

She said, "What are you going to do?"

"You're looking at the new head of the accounting department at Merrill Industries," he said.

She gave him a big hug and a kiss and said, "I am so happy for you,

I don't know what to say." Then she grew very quiet, and after a moment she said, "Elaine is here. Don't you feel it?"

He sat quietly for a moment with his eyes closed as if he were listening. Then he said, "Yes, you're right." It was the first time he had felt her presence.

Laura broke the silence saying, "Thank you, Elaine, for your part in all of this." Then as quickly as she had come she was gone. Ed and Laura sat there for a few minutes with tears in their eyes. Then they felt a great joy for the moment. Often after that they felt her presence in the garden at key moments in their lives, and they both realized that she was indeed looking after them somehow.

Ed started working at the plant the next week and marveled at the efficiency of the place. Merrill Industries functioned with the same efficiency as the products they made. Every new employee was made aware of the history of the company. John's father, Arthur, was one of those rare people who never saw a mechanical or electrical problem that he couldn't solve. With no formal education beyond high school, he had started his own business. He repaired radios and televisions and just about any other home appliance. But that wasn't enough. He started improving the designs of appliances he repaired. Then he started sending letters to the makers of the appliances telling how he could improve their products. Companies began calling him in for consultations on problems they were having. The business grew into a manufacturer of parts and supplies for the appliance manufacturers.

When his son, John, graduated from college with his business degree, he went to work on the business end of Merrill Industries, and soon it was as lean and efficient as the manufacturing end. When Ed started his new job, he found several ways to improve their accounting department and streamline their cash flow.

Over the years Ed began to move up the corporate ladder. He also became much more aware of the philosophy of the Merrills. The shelter wasn't their only charity. They were behind several local charities. They also were involved behind the scenes supporting civic projects. Ed began to be involved with some of these projects also. But the shelter was always his favorite. He rarely missed a day without visiting the shelter and walking through the garden with Laura. They often sat on their favorite bench discussing the future.

Then one Sunday when they were visiting Ed's parents, they were discussing buying a new home, and Ed's father said he would give them ten acres across the road next to the Blue River. When they left, they stopped and walked the grounds from the road to the river and fell in love with the idea of living there. They built a beautiful home on it that same year. Ed spent every spare minute at home working on the landscaping. They had an unobstructed view of the river from the back of the house, where the land sloped from the road to the river. Behind the house Ed created another garden. It wasn't walled, but was fenced with hedges and vine-covered arbors. Liz and Eli loved to play in the garden, and Liz asked if they could have a playhouse there. After some thought Ed built a miniature house in the back corner of the garden that looked as much like Elaine's cottage as he could remember.

As time went on and Ed moved up in Merrill Industries, he became known as one of the movers and shakers in Granville. Laura was the head of the Merrill Shelter, and her involvement in projects in the community put her in a position to improve many areas in the education and job-training organizations.

CHAPTER

24

Ed's father, Paul, was sitting at his desk looking at the records for the farm. He was no longer doing the farming himself. He was cash-renting his ground to his neighbor, who did all the farming and just rented the ground by the acre. He hadn't been feeling well since he got up that morning. He just felt out of sorts and was looking for something to do. As he was sitting at the desk, he felt a terrific pain in his chest. It was almost unbearable. He yelled for Rose. Then he passed out and slumped over the desk. When he came to, he couldn't figure out where he was. He was lying in a bed, and he was terribly uncomfortable. He turned his head and saw Rose sitting by his bedside. "Where am I?" he asked.

She was wiping tears from her eyes and said, "You are at Granville Medical. They said you have had a heart attack. They think you will be all right, but there has been some damage to your heart. Just get some rest, and you will feel better."

Ed had just walked out of a committee meeting when his secretary came to him and said he needed to get over to Granville Medical. His father had been brought in with a heart attack. When Ed walked into the emergency room, his father was just beginning to stabilize and they were taking him to a room where he could be monitored before sending him home. Ed and his mother sat in the room talking about what had happened while his father listened. Out of the blue he looked at Ed and said, "I'm scared. I don't think I will be leaving here, and I don't feel like I have led the life I should have."

Ed's mother began to weep and tried to reassure him that he was going to be fine and that he had led a great life. Ed sat in thought for a while, and then he said, "I am going to tell you something that I should have told you a long time ago, but I was afraid of what you would think." Then he told them about The Garden and his visit there with Elaine. "When your time comes," he told them, "Elaine will be waiting along with your parents and family members that you don't even know you have." Just as he finished telling them about The Garden, Laura walked into the room and apologized for not being able to get there sooner. Ed looked at her and said, "Laura, tell them about The Garden."

She looked at him and then at them and asked, "What have you told them?"

"Everything," he said.

She sat down and said, "It's true." Then she told them about Gabby and how he had led her into The Garden to where they found Ed and Elaine.

Ed took over, saying, "I don't know if we should have told you about this, but I don't want you to worry about dying. I would just as soon you didn't tell anyone else, because I realize most people wouldn't believe it. Anyway, they would just ask a lot of questions that I am not prepared to answer." Then he looked at his dad and said, "You will probably be here for years."

It was not to be, however. His dad died that night with Rose at his side. When Ed and Laura got back to the hospital, his mother was waiting calmly in the room holding his hand. She wept silently, and then, drying her eyes, she looked at them and said, "When he started struggling to get his breath, I felt as if Elaine was in the room with us, and he looked at me and smiled. Then he was gone." Ed's mother lived another two years, and then she too was gone. There wasn't anything wrong with her, and her health seemed to be fine; she just went to bed and it was over. A few years later Laura's father died, and her mother died shortly after.

CHAPTER

25

Soon Liz and Eli were off to college. As often as Ed could, he would walk down to the shelter to have lunch with Laura, and they always sat in the garden while they ate. There always seemed to be a peaceful atmosphere there. They talked about their problems and the kids, and they almost always talked as if Elaine was sitting there with them. Occasionally they would get the feeling that she was indeed there with them. Laura asked, "Do you ever go down to the bridge?"

"No," he replied, "I haven't been down there in years. Why?"

She hesitated, and then she almost looked guilty. "I go down there every once in a while. I guess I'm expecting to see The Garden, and I always hope I'll see Gabby making coffee by his fire. I did see Gabby one day, but he was walking down Sixth Street, and I didn't try to catch up to him. I felt like I would be interfering with something. He seemed to be in a hurry. I would like to sit down and talk to him about The Garden, but I don't suppose he could tell me much about it that we don't already know."

Ed thought about it for a while and then said, "I expect he could tell us a lot about it that we don't know, but I doubt he would want to talk about it."

Someone was coming down the path, and as they rounded a curve in the path they recognized Larry. He was older now and getting a little gray. "Hi, guys. I wondered if I would find you here. I walk through here about every week, but I don't want to bother you. Today I just felt like I would like to talk to you again. How are things going with you and the family? I was sorry to hear about your parents, Laura."

Laura smiled and asked, "How is your family?"

"Getting big," he said. "I've got one headed to college next year and one in high school."

"You seem to be doing pretty well in the construction business," Ed said. "I see your signs all over town."

"Yes, things are going real well, thanks to you guys."

"Tell me something," Ed said. "When you came by that day that I was trying to figure out how I was going to build this wall . . . was that an accident?"

Larry laughed. "Not really. I was down at the bridge talking to Gabby, and he told me what you were doing and told me I should stop by and see if I could help. It's a good thing he did. I think you would still be trying to figure it out."

Ed laughed, and then he thought of something that had never occurred to him before. "Had you ever seen a wall like this before that day?"

Larry looked a little embarrassed, and then he smiled and said, "I expect I saw the same one you did down under that bridge. You know how I was when I first came to town . . . I had a big chip on my shoulder and more than a few problems that I couldn't cope with. The first time I met Gabby, I tried to bully him into going into town to get me something to eat. He just looked at me and said, 'Here, have a cup of coffee. If you need something to eat, the Merrill Shelter is only a few blocks away, and they will feed you.' I knew from the look in his eye that this wasn't anyone I wanted to mess with.

"From that day on, we had several conversations about my life and what had put me on the streets. Then one day when he and I were alone, he told me that it was time to grow up and act like a man. He told me I was wasting my life and there was a lot that needed to be done. I made some kind of smart remark about why should I work my ass off just to be dropped into a hole in the ground for the effort. He looked me in the eye and said, 'Turn around and look behind you.' There it was, that beautiful wall and the garden behind it. I was dumbstruck. He said, 'The only way you will ever walk through that gate is if you get yourself together and earn your way.' I cried for the first time I could remember and asked him what I needed to do. That was the day he sent me to you. The funny thing is, I didn't really know what good it was going to do to build that wall. But when I saw the picture you showed me, I knew exactly what you had in mind. I couldn't build it to look like the real thing, but I could take my best stab at it, and I think it turned out pretty well.

"I only saw Gabby a couple of times after that. The last time I saw him was right after we finished the garden. I was walking down the path, and there he was sitting on a bench. I stopped to talk to him, and he told me what a great job we had done. You know, I had the weirdest feeling that he was there to put his seal of approval on the whole thing. I never felt the same after that when I walked through here. It felt even more special and peaceful after that. I never saw him after that, but I know that I will see him again when he opens that gate.

"I have absolutely no fear of death when it comes, because of him. I have tried to live my life the way I think he would have wanted me to, and I think that's why I have had the success I've had in business and in life. I always feel close to him when I walk through this garden. I almost feel as if he is giving me a nod of approval. I have often wondered if he wasn't just putting me on the path to success. Looking back, it's almost as if he had laid out a path for me to walk to get where I am today."

Ed's eyes were misty now, and he said, "I'm sure of it. I think he has done the same for us."

CHAPTER

26

Liz had met John Merrill's son Robert when they were both at day care. She hadn't paid that much attention to him at first, but they were always close friends. She couldn't remember the first time she had realized that she loved him. Robert felt as if he had always known. As far back as he could remember, he had looked forward every day to seeing her. They had gone through grade school and high school together, and when it came time to go to college, they had no doubt that they would both go to the same college. They dated all through college, and they both knew that after graduation they would be married.

Ed and Laura were sitting at the breakfast table when Liz came in and sat down. She looked almost aglow. "What?" Ed said.

She grinned and said, "Robert Merrill asked me to marry him."

Laura said, "Don't expect us to look surprised. Have you set the date yet?"

"We wanted to tell you and his parents before we did that. What do you think?"

Laura teared up and said, "I think it's a perfect match."

They looked at Ed, and he hesitated a second before he broke into a smile and said he thought so too. They both hugged her, and Ed laughed and said, "What is this going to cost me?"

They had the wedding in the garden at the river house, and it seemed like the entire town was there. When Robert and Liz returned from their honeymoon, Ed asked them where they were going to live. Liz said they would be looking for a place in Granville. Robert would be working for Merrill Industries, and she was going to work at the shelter with Laura.

"When did that happen?" Ed asked her. She said Robert had talked to his dad, and he had set everything up. Laura was excited about working with Liz and was already trying to rearrange job assignments to see where she would fit in the best. Ed said, "Would you consider building a place next to us? I will give you the ten acres next to us if you want to consider it."

Liz looked at Robert, and he laughed. "She told me you would do this," he said.

Laura said, "Well, what do you think?"

Robert said, "We would love it. I don't know how to thank you." He hugged Laura and shook Ed's hand and said, "I hope you will help us with the garden. Liz never stops talking about growing up playing in your garden." Robert and Liz started looking for house plans the next day. Two months later they started construction. The next spring they started on the garden, with Liz directing the planning. Ed and Laura were surprised at how much thought she had put into the planning of the house and garden.

CHAPTER

27

That fall Liz announced that she was pregnant. When the big day came, Ed and Laura were in the waiting room when Robert came in to announce they were the grandparents of a girl. "What are you going to call her?" Laura asked.

"Liz told me she wanted to tell you." He looked a little puzzled about why she wanted to do it this way. "Go on in and see your new grandchild," he said, "I will wait here."

When they got into her room, Liz was smiling from ear to ear. "All right, what is the big mystery?" Ed asked.

"Yes, tell us," said Laura.

Liz pulled the blanket back and said, "Meet your new granddaughter, Elaine."

They had never talked about Elaine to the children, and they were stunned. Laura started to cry and asked, "How did you decide on the name?"

Liz said, "Mom, don't you remember my doll Ellie when I was little?"

Laura said, "Yes, but I don't understand."

"Well, I called her Ellie, but her name was Elaine."

"Why did you name your doll Elaine?" Ed asked.

Liz said, "When I was playing in the playhouse in the garden, I had an imaginary friend and she told me her name was Elaine."

Ed asked her, "When she was there, could you actually see her, or was it just in your imagination?"

Liz said, "That's hard to say. I could see her, and at first I thought she was really there, but she would be gone for long periods of time, so I thought I was just imagining it." When she described her friend, Ed and Laura could only look at her in amazement. "What's wrong?" Liz asked. "You look like you've seen a ghost."

"Tell us more about Elaine," they asked.

"Well, she lived in the playhouse, and sometimes when I was playing there she came to see me. She told me she would visit me from time to time, but it was our little secret. She wasn't always there when I wanted to talk. I was always surprised when she was there. When I got older, she stopped coming, but it all seemed so real when she did come. I have never told anyone about her until now.

"A strange thing happened when I was in delivery. I thought I could hear her comforting me, but when I looked around, she wasn't there." Ed and Laura stood there looking at each other for what seemed like hours. Finally Liz said, "What is wrong? You haven't said a word about what I just told you."

Ed took her hand and said, "Listen, honey, you can't say a word about what I am going to tell you." Then he told her the whole story about Elaine and the accident and The Garden.

It was Liz's turn to be silent. Then she shed a few tears and said, "A lot of things are starting to make some kind of sense to me now . . . things she said to me when I was little that I didn't really understand."

Then Ed had a thought. "Where was Eli when she visited you?"

"Sometimes he was there, but he promised he would keep it a secret too."

"Well," Ed said, "I think maybe we should all keep her secret. You realize what people would think if we told anyone about this?"

Liz smiled. "I guess you could call it a family secret, right?"

"Have you said anything to Robert about Elaine?" Ed asked.

"No," she said, "I'm not sure what he would think about it."

"Well," Ed said, "I will leave that up to you. You will know when and if you should bring this up."

Two weeks later Ed and Laura had Robert and Liz over for dinner. Before they came, Ed rummaged through some old things he had in a closet and found a package of old family pictures. There were several pictures of Elaine either alone or standing next to Ed or their parents. He took them down and arranged them on the kitchen table. When Robert and Liz arrived, he waited until Laura was busy with the baby and talking to Robert, and then he asked Liz to come into the kitchen. He asked her if she knew who any of the people in the pictures were. She was looking at them and gasped. She picked one up and said, "This is Elaine."

Then Ed went out and got Eli and asked him to come into the kitchen. When he showed him the pictures on the table, he asked him if he recognized anyone. Eli picked up a picture of Elaine and said, "I know her." Then he told them about Elaine and the playhouse and how he and Liz use to talk to her. Ed explained who she was and what had happened to her and Michael and Teresa. Eli asked him, "Why haven't you told us about this before? I didn't know you had been married before."

"It was just too painful," he said. "And even now I don't like to talk about it. But you are old enough now to understand, and I really can't explain about Elaine, except to say that I think she has been watching out for all of us for a long time."

Liz looked at Ed and said, "I think I am going to tell Robert about all of this tonight, so he may be asking you about it the next time he sees you."

Laura had been in the living room talking to Robert, and she came into the kitchen and asked what was going on. Then she saw the pictures on the table, and she looked at Ed and said, "What is this all about?" He explained what had happened, and she was floored.

When she had recovered herself, she looked at Liz and said, "You had better go in with Robert; he is sitting in there with the baby alone. He might be wondering what is going on out here."

Liz nodded and said, "We are going to have to sit down and talk about this some more, and we will have to include Robert in the conversation. I am going to talk to him about this tonight."

When Robert and Liz got home that evening, Liz said, "We have to sit down and talk. I have something to tell you, and I don't know how you are going to take it. I wouldn't believe it myself if I wasn't a part of it." She started at the beginning when she first encountered Elaine in the playhouse, and she told him everything that had happened up to when she saw the pictures tonight.

When she had finished, Robert was quiet for a while. Then he said, "I wouldn't have believed it if anyone but you had told me this. But I also know your parents well enough to know that they wouldn't make up something like this. Let me think about this for a while, and then we will talk to your parents about it."

She smiled and said, "I knew you would respond this way. We are supposed to go to Mom and Dad's tomorrow night to talk about it. Today is the first time we have ever talked about this as a family. I had no idea that my parents knew anything about Elaine until they visited me in the hospital. Tomorrow afternoon I would like to go out to the Granville cemetery and visit the graves of Elaine, Michael, and Teresa. Robert, I hope you are not going to say anything about this to anyone."

He laughed. "Don't worry. I won't. Who would believe it?"

The next afternoon they visited the cemetery. As they stood there looking at the headstone, Liz wept and then took Robert's arm and said, "Elaine is here. I feel her presence."

He took her hand and said, "I don't know if I feel her presence, but the hair started standing up on the back of my neck just before you said that."

She stood silent for a while as if she were listening to someone, and then she said, "Tonight should be interesting."

They were gathered in the living room before dinner. Liz started the conversation by telling them that she and Robert had visited the cemetery that afternoon. Ed said, "It has been quite a while since I've been there. I should visit more often." Then he looked at Robert and asked what he thought about all of this.

Robert said, "I was pretty unnerved when Liz told me about it last night, but I knew she wouldn't make something like that up. Today at the cemetery she told me she could feel Elaine there, and I felt a little weird myself, although I didn't see or hear her."

Ed looked at Liz and asked, "Does that mean that you did see her?"

"No, I didn't see her, but I did hear her voice. I didn't tell Robert what she said, but I think it is a message for you, Dad. She said not to worry, but she has something to discuss with you and will see you soon."

Ed sat down, and his eyes filled. "I hope there isn't anything wrong. I can't imagine what she means that I will be seeing her soon."

CHAPTER

28

Ed woke with a start. He lay in the dark trying to figure out what had awakened him. At first he thought Laura had said his name, but she was sleeping. Then he heard it again. It was very soft but clear. *Ed!* It didn't seem to come from within the room. He got up and looked out the window and froze. There in the yard was The Garden wall. He thought, *I must be dreaming*, but there was his bed with Laura still sleeping. He quickly pulled on his clothes and went downstairs and out onto the patio. The Garden was there before him, and right in front of him was the open gate. He looked around for Gabby, but he was nowhere in sight. Then he heard his name again and realized it was Elaine's voice and it was coming from within The Garden. He hesitated for a second and then entered The Garden. He walked through the gate and heard the soft click behind him and felt the cold run through his body. Now he was comfortable and felt the same relaxed, peaceful feeling he had experienced the first time he had entered The Garden.

He walked along the path, and everything seemed as familiar as if it had been only yesterday that he had last been here. As he walked around the first turn in the path, there was Elaine sitting on a bench waiting for him. As he approached, she rose and came to him smiling, as beautiful as ever. She gave him a big hug and a kiss and turned back to the bench. He sat beside her trying to think what to say. Finally he asked, "What am I doing here"?

She looked at him with a sad smile on her face and said, "I need your help."

"Anything," he replied.

She was silent for a minute, and then she said, "Teresa is in trouble, and I haven't been able to help her. You know that I have kept watch over the children all of these years to see that they were all right."

"Yes," he said, "and evidently you were looking after Eli and Liz too." She laughed and said, "They told you about me, did they?"

"You know they did," he said. "When Liz named her daughter Elaine, we were amazed because we had never talked to the children about you. When we asked her where she came up with your name, she explained the whole thing about you in the garden when they were playing in their cottage."

"I hope you don't mind, but I just felt like I should be a part of their lives," she said. "What did Laura think about it?"

"I think she thought it was wonderful," he said.

"Okay, what kind of trouble is Teresa in and what do I need to do?" he asked.

"Well, let me say that it isn't an emergency. She isn't in physical danger or anything like that, but she is so worried and afraid of her situation that I can't reach her. She was married, and her husband, Tom, died suddenly. She has a daughter, five years old, and they lost everything when Tom died. She is trying to work and take care of her daughter, but all she can find are part-time jobs that don't pay enough to take care of her day care. She is waiting tables in a café, and she just can't make it on what she is earning. She is behind in her rent and all of her bills. Her daughter's name is Sarah, by the way.

"She has an education, but when she got married and pregnant, she became a stay-at-home mom. Now she needs to get a job, and she doesn't have anyone to turn to. Having been out of school for the last few years, she isn't current on the things that would make her a good hire. Her parents are having health problems and can't really give her the kind of help she needs, and Tom's parents were never supportive of the marriage to begin with, and they don't live close enough to help."

Ed looked at her and said, "Don't worry. I'll take care of it."

Elaine said, "I knew you would. I have tried everything to help her, but there is a limit to what I can do by trying to put thoughts into her head. One thing that I kept trying to get her to do was put in an application at Merrill Industries, and I think she either has already done it or is going to."

"That's great. I'll check with Human Resources and watch for her application.

"Tell me, what about Michael? How is he doing?"

"He is doing great; he is an aircraft mechanic by trade. He works for Granville Aeronautics, and he has just about taken over the running of the entire operation there. He is one of those people who love what they do, so they do it extremely well . . . sort of like someone else I know." She smiled at him, and he couldn't help giving her a hug and a kiss.

Ed asked, "Can you tell me his name?"

"Yes, it is Troy Purcell, but you can never let him know about us."

"I know," he said, "but I can make sure he is all right too."

Then Elaine said, "About Teresa . . . her name is Carolyn Ingrahm. I guess I don't need to tell you this, Ed, but you can't tell anyone about this. Most of all, Carolyn."

Ed laughed and said, "I know; this one is between us."

Elaine gave him a little smile, and he said, "All right, what else?" ""Nothing," she said. "I just want you to know that everything is going well, and I'm happy."

Ed hesitated, a little unsure of how to bring it up, but then he looked at her and asked, "Have you found anyone else to share your life with here?"

She put her arms around him and said, "I'll never find anyone else like you, so why would I look?"

He laughed and then turned serious. "I've thought about you often, and I hate to think of you being alone."

"But I'm not alone," she said. "I have our entire families around me, and I keep so busy I don't have time to feel lonely."

A thought struck him, and he looked at her and asked, "Do you know how long I have before I come to The Garden to stay?"

"Not for quite a while. I don't know when; I just know it won't be soon. But I'll be waiting for you and Laura when the time comes."

CHAPTER

29

Laura woke when the radio came on. When she rolled over to nudge Ed, he was already up. *Strange,* she thought. *I didn't hear him get up.* She got up and got ready for work, expecting him to come in at any time to see if she was getting ready. When he hadn't come upstairs by the time she was finished, she was really puzzled. Then she noticed that the clothes he had laid out for work today were still there on their hangers. She went down to the kitchen and started coffee and called for him. Now she was worried; he had to be there somewhere. She started out the door to the patio and gasped. There was The Garden. Then she heard an old familiar voice say, "Good morning." She spun around, and there sat Gabby at the patio table smiling at her. He said, "Am I too early for a cup of coffee?"

She sat down completely taken aback. "What is going on?" she asked.

Gabby just looked at her and said, "I can't tell you anything without a cup of coffee."

Now it was Laura's turn to laugh, and she said, "Coming right up."

When they had the coffee, they sat down and Gabby said, "We are going to meet Ed in about fifteen minutes, and you are probably going to be late for work again."

CHAPTER

30

Ed and Elaine walked back to the gate. When they were almost there, Ed realized that there were people sitting on the bench just inside the gate. As they approached the bench, Laura and Gabby got up and walked toward them. He looked at Elaine and asked, "What's going on?"

She said, "When I said you couldn't tell anyone about this, I didn't mean Laura. She has been here before, and we know she will keep all of this to herself." As Gabby and Laura walked up, Elaine hugged Laura and said, "I think we need to take another walk."

They walked off, leaving Gabby and Ed looking at each other. Ed turned to Gabby and asked, "Do you know what that is all about?"

Gabby watched as they walked down the path, and he said, "I think Elaine is going to ask Laura how she feels about all of this and maybe how she might help."

As they walked along the path, Elaine turned to Laura and said, "I have asked Ed to help Teresa. She is having some trouble, and Ed was the only person I could turn to. Her name is Carolyn now, and she is alone and in a bit of financial trouble. I hope you don't mind my having Ed get involved with helping Carolyn. She needs help, and nothing I have done seems to help."

Laura gave her a hug and said, "Not at all. I hope I can help as well. I'm sure we can handle things discreetly, and we will do whatever we can."

Elaine looked at her and seemed at a loss for words. Then she said, "Thank you, but I have something else that I need to talk to you about, and I'm afraid of what your response might be. Let's sit down for a while and see how you feel about what I have to say. You have seen how things are here in The Garden, and I have something I would like for you to think about. I've never had a sister, but I think it must feel just like it is between the two of us. I don't know of an easy way to approach this, so I will just come to the point. What would you think if, when the time comes, Ed and you and I were to live together?"

Laura looked dumbstruck. "I don't know," she said. "Do you mean like husband and wives?"

Elaine smiled and said, "Yes, that is what I mean." She put her hand on Laura's arm and said, "I am sorry. I've upset you, and I shouldn't have presented this to you so suddenly."

"No, no . . ." Laura brushed tears from her eyes and said, "It did give me quite a start, but I have to tell you that I have thought about what would happen when we returned to The Garden. I have never mentioned it to Ed, but I have worried about how he would feel about me once he had returned to The Garden. He loved you first, and knowing him, that love is just as strong as it ever was. I can't bear to think that I would lose him, and it has cost me a lot of sleepless nights."

Now it was Elaine's turn to tear up. "Look," she said, "I have had the same thoughts about you. The fact is he loves both of us. That's why I brought this up. There doesn't have to be a choice. This is not uncommon in The Garden. A lot of people who have remarried after the loss of a loved one face the same dilemma when they come here. The problem here isn't who loves whom the most. The question is, Can we share that love?"

Laura was quiet for several seconds. Then she turned to Elaine and gave her a big hug. "I think I have loved you like a sister since my first visit to The Garden. In some ways this conversation has put me at ease. Give me some time to think about this. I can't imagine what Ed will think."

Elaine said, "I think it will come as a bit of a shock to him, but I also think he has probably had a few sleepless nights thinking about this, just as we have. I should tell you that I was already aware of the feelings between you and Ed before either of you visited The Garden the first time . . . probably before either of you knew the extent of your feelings for each other. I have to tell you that I was very happy for you and Ed, but I also had a feeling of loss. If you decide to have a conversation about this with Ed, I would like for you to do something for me. Take him to the garden at the shelter when you two can be alone, and I will come. Now I think we should get back; I expect Ed is wondering what we have been doing for so long."

CHAPTER

31

The girls had been gone for quite a while, and when they were walking back, Ed was struck by how much alike they seemed. He had never noticed how much alike their walk and gestures were. As they approached, he also realized how much he and Laura had aged. Not that they didn't know it, but the first time they had been in The Garden, Laura and Elaine could have been sisters. Now Laura could pass for Elaine's mother. He was having trouble with his feelings about the two of them. He felt the same love for both of them, and yet it was different. He couldn't love Laura more; she had been with him through the darkest of times. She was the rock that had kept him going when others would have discouraged him. At the same time he knew that Elaine had been the guiding hand that had made his and Laura's life together the miraculous thing that it was.

When Elaine and Laura got closer they were smiling, but Ed could tell that they had both been crying. He had spent many a night staring at the ceiling wondering what it was going to be like when he and Laura were both in The Garden. He would be seeing Elaine and Laura together, and it seemed to him that it would be pretty awkward. Gabby turned to them and said, "Say your good-byes; it is time to go."

Laura turned to Elaine and said, "Don't worry; everything is going to be all right." She hugged Elaine and said, "Thank you for all you have done for us. You are always in my thoughts and prayers." In a lower voice she said, "We'll talk soon."

Ed turned to Elaine and took her in his arms and kissed her. "We will take care of everything. Teresa's life is about to change for the better, and I promise she will never know why." Ed turned and took Laura by the hand,

and they followed Gabby back to the gate. Elaine followed along. At the gate they said their good-byes, and Ed and Laura turned and walked out of The Garden. They heard the gate click, and when they turned back, they were looking across fields at the river behind their house.

CHAPTER

32

Ed and Laura were both late for work. When Ed got to his office, he immediately called Molly at Human Resources and asked her if they had an application on file for a Carolyn Ingraham. After a short pause she said, "Yes, she applied day before yesterday. Frankly, Ed, she seems to be a bit overqualified for anything we have openings for."

Ed told her that a friend had recommended Carolyn. Then Ed asked, "Would you mind if I interviewed her? I know it's a bit unusual, but I sort of promised."

Molly laughed and said, "Ed, you don't even have to ask. I'll send you a copy of her resume and application, and set up a meeting with her as soon as her schedule will permit."

When Carolyn got home from the cafe, the apartment manager told her she had had a call from Merrill Industries and that she was to call them. She called right away, and the woman asked when she could come in for an interview. "I can come anytime you want me," she replied. Molly scheduled her for the next morning. When Molly confirmed her appointment, Ed went through her resume and application to see what her background was. Then he went through their list of job vacancies to see if he could come up with a match. The department head in shipping was asking for someone to replace his retiring secretary. Ed looked at the pay scale and Carolyn's qualifications and decided she could be a good fit if she didn't mind taking a job that she was clearly overqualified for. If she did well, he would keep a lookout for opportunities to move her up to better-paying jobs.

When it got close to the time for her interview, Ed was both nervous and excited to see Carolyn. He hoped they would hit it off and at the same time realized that he couldn't make his feelings obvious.

CHAPTER

33

Carolyn was so nervous she was practically shaking. She needed this job no matter what it paid. She knew that if she could get on and do a good job, she would be able to make a decent living. Molly was very friendly and walked her to Ed's office. Ed's secretary buzzed him and told him his interview was here, and showed her into his office. As Carolyn was walking into the office, she noticed a plaque on the door that said, "Ed Williams, Vice President, Finance." Now she was really nervous, but when Ed came around his desk smiling and shook her hand, she suddenly felt very relaxed. She knew she had never met this man before, but she also knew that he seemed familiar. He explained that she was clearly overqualified for the job they were offering her, but if she wanted to try it, she was hired. "If you take the job, I can't promise you how long it will be before something more in line with your qualifications comes along."

Carolyn was blinking back tears. "I will take it without even knowing what it pays," she said. "I really need the job. I'm a single mother with a daughter. My husband died, and I have to make a life for my daughter."

Ed told her what she would be paid and added, "You will also have company-paid health insurance, paid vacations, and a retirement program."

Carolyn was floored. Now she did start to cry. Ed handed her a tissue, and as she wiped her eyes she said, "Now I'm embarrassed. I'm sorry, but this is a bit overwhelming. I've been living on what I could make waiting tables. Now I can afford day care and give Sarah the kind of security she should have."

Ed was on the verge of tears himself. He walked around the desk and put his arm on her shoulder. He said, "I understand, and there is nothing to be embarrassed about. Come with me down to the second floor. I want to show you our day-care center. If you like it, you won't need to pay for day care. We provide it for our employees."

When he had shown her around the center, she said, "This is perfect. I can see her during lunch."

Ed smiled and said, "You can drop in on her anytime you have some free time. When can you start"?

"Immediately," she said. "All I have to do is call the restaurant, and they can get one of the other girls to take my shift."

Ed said, "Report here at eight tomorrow morning, and bring Sarah with you. The receptionist will take you to Shipping and introduce you to your new boss. His secretary is getting ready to retire, and she will be able to get you trained before she leaves."

When Carolyn got home that evening, she was walking on air. The future that had looked so bleak now looked bright with promise. She felt like she would sleep better that night than she had in months. Then in those early morning hours between sound sleep and wakefulness, an old dream came back. There was the beautiful blond and the tall man that she had dreamed of when she was very small. When she got up the next morning, something in the back of her mind still bothered her. She couldn't quite put her finger on what was bothering her; she knew it was a dream, but she couldn't quite remember what she had dreamed.

CHAPTER

34

Ed couldn't wait to get back to the office to call Laura. He told her everything about the interview, and she said, "I think I will go in with you in the morning, and maybe we can time it to be in the reception area when she comes in so I can meet her."

The next morning they were talking to the receptionist when Carolyn and Sarah came in. Ed introduced Laura to Carolyn, and Laura welcomed her to Merrill Industries. "Why don't I walk you up to the day-care center, and then I'll take you down to Shipping," she said. She told Ed good-bye and gave him a wink and walked Carolyn and Sarah up to the center.

Carolyn asked her, "Do you work here too?"

"No," said Laura. "I work over at the Merrill Shelter, but I spend enough time over here to know most of the people working here."

"I've been there a few times," Carolyn said. "I like to walk in the garden there. It is so peaceful, and I like to sit there and think."

Laura said, "I'm surprised I haven't seen you there. Ed and I spend a lot of time in the garden. We like to sit there and work out problems, and you're right—it is a peaceful place. Did you know that Ed built the walls around the garden? It was his idea to have a garden there at the shelter. He was working there before he came here. The Merrills are very good people. They finance the shelter and several other community projects. You are going to love it here. It is a very employee-friendly company."

That night when Ed and Laura got home from work, they talked about Carolyn and Sarah, and how they would handle their relationship. Then Ed asked her, "What did you and Elaine talk about when you went for your walk in The Garden?"

Laura laughed. "Well, it's something you and I will have to talk about, but not now. I think maybe tomorrow evening in the shelter garden. Come by after work, and we'll go out for a bite to eat. Then I want to talk to you in the garden. We did talk about Carolyn, and she wanted to know how I felt about your stepping in to help out."

"Well, how do you feel?" he asked.

She said, "After all Elaine has done for us, I am really happy that we can do something in return. Now, how can we pull Carolyn closer to our family without making her feel like we are taking over her life?" Then she brightened and said, "I know how to do it. Robert and Liz take Elly to the day-care center at Merrill's. If Elly and Sarah were to develop a friendship, we could invite them here for Elly and Sarah to play together. They are about the same age. It could work."

"That sounds good, but we can't let Liz and the kids know what we're doing. We can't let them ever know their true relationship."

"Okay, I'll tell you what. You leave it to me, and I think Elaine will have something to do with it also."

"You will have to explain that to me," Ed said.

"We will talk about that tomorrow night too," she said.

The next day when Laura was at the shelter and had some time, she walked out into the garden and went to her favorite bench in a secluded corner. As she sat there, she was thinking about Carolyn and Sarah and how she hoped to get them to become fast friends. Then she felt the hair on her neck rise, and she became very relaxed and comfortable. She knew this feeling. Elaine was here. Laura didn't know if she had actually spoken the words or just thought them. "Elaine, Ed and I will be here tonight. I haven't told him about our conversation in The Garden. I would like for you to be here too. Maybe I just need moral support, but I think this needs to be between the three of us. We can also bring you up to date on Carolyn and Sarah. We think Sarah and Elly can become the best of friends. They are in the Merrill day-care center together, and we would like them to become friends. That way, we will have an excuse to bring them closer to our family. We feel like Carolyn needs a familial relationship, and this is the only way we know how to go about it."

Then she felt, more than she heard, the reply. *I will talk to Sarah about Elly. Starting tonight I will try to plant the idea in her sleep.*

"We keep you in our thoughts and prayers," Laura said.

I'll be here tonight, Elaine replied.

Then she was gone, and Laura realized that she had never felt so at peace . . . not just because of the presence of Elaine, but because of the knowledge of The Garden. She was comforted by the thought of there being a familiar world on the other side of that gate. She knew that when her time came, Gabby would be there waiting to escort her into The Garden and the next phase of her life.

She was just getting ready to go back to work when Ed walked up and sat with her. He looked at her and said, "What's happened? You look incredibly happy." She explained what had happened and how she felt about it. He thought how strange it was that he hadn't really connected The Garden with his own death. While he knew that was what would happen, he hadn't felt the peace of that knowing. Now it washed over him, and he held Laura and they sat there for a long time contemplating what it would mean.

"What are you doing here now?" she asked. "I thought we had a date tonight."

"I haven't been able to concentrate all day," he said. "I just thought I would walk over and sit here in the garden and try to think things out. It's always worked for me before. I have a lot of things on my mind that I can't seem to resolve."

"Well," she said, "I need to get back to work, and I will see you here this evening."

CHAPTER

35

After dinner they walked back to the shelter and went into the garden.

Laura said, "I think you need to sit down and get comfortable. We have something to discuss, and this is the best place I know of to discuss it. Have you ever thought about what will happen when we return to The Garden? I have, and it has cost me a lot of sleepless nights."

Ed was very quiet for few seconds, and then he said, "I have to say that I have lost a little sleep over it myself. It seems to me that it could be a bit awkward with both of us being there where we could see Elaine. We could live somewhere far away from her, but we would still see her from time to time. I can't say that I don't love her anymore. I will always love her, but I also love you, and I wouldn't want you to think for one minute that I could choose her over you. It just isn't possible." He looked at Laura to see if he had hurt her or upset her.

He was surprised to see that she was smiling at him. "I have bit of a surprise for you," she said. They looked at each other, and then they both reached out to hold hands. They both knew that feeling. They looked up, and Elaine was standing there. They both felt a shock. This was the first time they had seen Elaine appear outside The Garden. Laura was the first to recover, and she said, "Hello, Elaine. You are right on time. We didn't expect to be able to see you, though."

Elaine laughed and said, "I thought with what we are here to discuss, it might be more comfortable if you could see me. This is the first time I've been visible outside The Garden since I came to visit Eli and Liz."

Ed suddenly felt a little puzzled and uncomfortable. "What's this about?" he asked.

Laura took Ed's hand and related the conversation she and Elaine had had in The Garden. Ed started to say something, but Laura stopped him. "Elaine," she said, "I have thought about this for hours, and I think it is the only sensible solution. She looked at Ed and asked, "What do you think?"

Ed was both confused and relieved. "I can't say that I haven't lain awake for many a night thinking about this, and I never could come to a solution. But I wouldn't do anything to hurt either of you. Elaine, I missed you terribly, as you know. It almost destroyed me, but you and Laura pulled me back from an abyss. I don't know how to separate my love for the two of you. I am the luckiest of men to have known two great loves with two of the best women I have ever known. This isn't a decision I can make if it means hurting either of you. At the same time, I feel like I could be hurting both of you by not making that decision."

Elaine interrupted. "Laura and I have discussed this, and, believe me, we know that this a difficult thing to even think about, but you are not going to hurt us if you don't think you can choose us both. But I also have to tell you that the love of neither of us would be diminished if you decide between us. I told Laura that this is not uncommon in The Garden. Many people remarry after the loss of a loved one and are then reunited after death. Most find that it works very well if the two partners like each other. Laura and I have professed that we love each other like sisters, and we both agree that we think we can make this work."

Ed squeezed Laura's hand and said, "Let me think about this and talk it over with Laura. It may be that I will have to wait until that day comes when I return to The Garden before I know if this is something that I can do. I hope you don't think that I hesitate because I love one of you more than the other. That couldn't be further from the truth. I love you both deeply. I'm just going to have to let this play out in my mind. Before you go, Elaine, I don't know how much Laura has told you, but we have Carolyn working at Merrill's, and we are going to work her and Sarah into our family. We will take care of them."

Elaine said, "I will leave you now. I know that you will take good care of them. Remember that whatever you decide about us, Laura and I will always love you." Then she was gone as suddenly as she had come.

Laura looked at Ed and said, "I am all right with this if you decide to do it. Elaine and I are as close as two people can be with each other. I don't need to know what you decide; I will be happy no matter what."

CHAPTER

36

A few days later, after a meeting with John Merrill, Ed asked, "Don't you keep the company plane at the Granville Airport?"

John said, "Sure. Why do you ask?"

"I don't know . . . I knew you had one, and I never thought about where you kept it, I guess."

"Well, it hadn't been used much until recently when we started expanding our sales network. Now we use it quite a bit," John said. "I have to go out there and talk to the maintenance people tomorrow. Would you like to come out and see it?"

"Sure," Ed said.

The next morning they drove out, and John took Ed into the hangar. "We just had the engines overhauled," he said. "We like to keep it in tip-top shape, what with all the time we've been putting on it. I have to talk to the chief mechanic, Troy, about it and see how much it is going to set us back."

They walked into the office, and Troy was on the phone and waved them to a couple of chairs. Ed was studying him carefully and thought about Michael. There was no resemblance he could see, but then he hadn't really expected there to be any. When Troy got off the phone, he came around the desk and shook hands with John and Ed. He looked at Ed and said, "Have we met before? You look familiar."

John said, "This is Ed Williams, our vice president of finance. You may have seen him on TV; he has had several interviews about our company. He hasn't seen our plane, and I thought I would bring him out to see it . . . especially since he is going to get the bills."

Troy laughed and said, "It won't be cheap; we have put those engines in perfect condition. I worked on it all week, and we finished it up last night. Let's go out and look it over."

As they walked around the plane, Troy explained what they had done to it. Ed was surprised at how much of it he understood. It was much more complicated than the farm equipment he had worked on as a boy. He was surprised at how enjoyable it was to be around machinery again. John was asking questions about it and seemed to be pretty familiar with what had been done.

Ed asked Troy, "I understand you are the chief mechanic. Do you fly too?"

"Oh, sure. I learned to fly before I started training for my A&P. I like to be able to take them up after I've worked on them to make sure they are performing the way they're supposed to."

"What does A&P mean?" Ed asked.

"It's airframe and power plant," Troy replied. "You have to be licensed to work on the airframe and engines if you want to be able to work on the whole plane."

"That sounds like something that would take pretty intensive training. What kind of education do you have to have for something like that?"

"In college I studied aeronautical engineering and business management, but I like to get my hands dirty, so the logical thing to me was to learn how to repair and maintain aircraft."

"Well, it looks like you have found your niche. Do you like it here?"

"Yes, I do. I look forward to coming in every day. We have quite a bit of traffic here for a relatively small airport, and hardly a day goes by that we don't get someone with some problem for us to look into."

John said, "Well, Ed, it looks like we need to get back to the grind. Send the bill to Ed, Troy. He's the one that will end up with it anyway."

After they had left, Troy was puzzled at the feelings he had about Ed. He tried to remember where he had met him before, but nothing came to him. He was sure that he hadn't seen him on television, but he couldn't place him anywhere else either. There was something that stirred in the back of his mind, but, try as he might, he couldn't bring it into focus.

That night Ed told Laura about meeting Troy. "He seems to be getting along pretty well, but I would still like to do something for him, even if he doesn't know who did it."

Laura gave him a little grin and said, "Let me see what I can come up with. I'll look into it tomorrow."

Ed said, "He gave me a little bit of a start this morning. When we were introduced, he wanted to know if we had met before. He thought I looked familiar. John bailed me out without even knowing it. He said, 'You have probably seen him on TV. He has been interviewed about the company.'"

She said, "What do you think? Does he remember you but just can't figure out why?"

Ed thought about it for a second and said, "I'm afraid he does remember me, but of course he can't make that connection. It would be too great a leap. After all, how many times have you seen someone that looked familiar to you but you couldn't make a connection? You may have seen the person anywhere before and just couldn't remember where."

"It's happened to me a lot. Now I have to wonder if this isn't my second time here." They both laughed about that, but it did give them both something to wonder about.

The next day Laura got out the Granville City Directory and looked up Troy Purcell. He was married and had two children. His wife's name was Mary. When she looked up Mary Purcell, she was surprised to see that she worked for Larry Ellison Contracting. Larry was one of Ed's oldest friends. He had helped Ed build the wall around the Merrill Shelter. She called Larry's office. She was trying to figure out how to tell Larry what she wanted to do, when he answered. When Larry answered, she said, "Hi, Larry. This is Laura Williams. How are you and the family?"

Larry said, "Hi, Laura. Everything is going great with us. How is everything with you and your family?"

"Great," she said. "Everyone is doing real well. Listen, I don't quite know how to go about this, but do you have someone named Mary Purcell working for you?"

"Sure, she is practically running the place. She isn't here right now; she's out doing an estimate for me. Do you want me to have her call you?"

"No, don't tell her I called. Look, I don't know quite how to explain this, but it has to do with The Garden."

There was a pause, and then Larry said, "Okay, I understand . . . I think."

"Great," Laura said. "Ed and I want to do something for her and her husband, Troy, but we don't know what they could use. I have an idea. Could you arrange to have Mary come out to the house to look over our garden and give us some ideas for what we could do with it? I'm not sure we actually are going to do anything, but she could look it over and give us an estimate. While she's here, maybe I could talk to her and get some ideas."

Larry laughed and said, "I don't know why you women aren't running the world. You're downright diabolical."

Laura laughed and said, "What makes you think we aren't running it?"

"Now you've got me worried," he said. "When would you like for her to come?"

"Does she work on Saturdays?"

"In this business you work whenever the customer needs you," he said.

"Great. Anytime Saturday works for us."

When she got home, Ed was puttering around in the garden. She said, "I'm thinking about having some work done in the garden."

Ed looked at her and said, "Why? What's wrong with it? I do all the work that needs to be done out here."

Laura grinned and said, "Mary Purcell works for Larry Ellison, and she is coming out Saturday to look it over and give me an estimate."

Ed looked at her for a minute and then broke out laughing. "I don't know how you do these things, but you scare me."

Saturday morning at about ten they were sitting on the patio when Mary arrived. Laura and Ed showed her the garden and asked her for suggestions about what they could do to improve it. She said, "You've got a beautiful place here. I'm not sure I can improve it much, but let me look it over, and I'll see what I can come up with." An hour later she had some ideas for them. Ed started to look interested. He was asking her questions about plants and concrete work and some of the things that she had suggested.

Laura asked her if she had time to have some coffee. "I've just taken a coffee cake out of the oven, and it's more than the two of us can eat."

Mary laughed and said, "It sounds pretty good. I was in such a rush this morning that I skipped breakfast."

The three of them sat and talked about the garden, and Mary said, "I really envy you being able to live in a place like this. Troy and I are trying to find a place out away from the city to build. This is just beautiful."

Ed said, "Troy? Does your husband work at the airport?"

"Yes," she said. "Do you know him?"

"Actually, I met him this week," he said. "I work for Merrill Industries, and I was out there with John Merrill. John wanted to talk to Troy about what they had done with the company airplane."

Laura poured some more coffee and asked if they wanted some more coffee cake. Mary hesitated and then said, "It is pretty good . . . maybe one more piece."

"Where are you thinking about building?" Laura asked.

"Well, we aren't sure. We have looked at several places, but the banks aren't too keen to lend money on building lots right now. We would like to have the ground bought before we list our house so that we could start construction and finish the new house as soon as possible after we listed."

"Have you looked out here in this area?" she asked.

"No, I've driven by here a few times going to jobs, but I haven't seen anything for sale, and I'm not sure we could buy anything larger than maybe an acre." They talked for a while longer, and then Mary said, "I had better get going. Let me look over my notes, and I can send you some sketches and an estimate."

"Thanks a lot," Laura said. "We will look them over and let you know what we decide."

When Mary had left, Laura looked at Ed and said, "Well, what do you think?"

Ed looked puzzled. "What do I think about what?"

"Look," she said, "how much ground do we own along the river here?"

Ed perked up. "About two hundred acres with what we inherited when dad died. What are you thinking?"

She looked at him and said, "Why don't we offer them about ten acres right next to ours at a really good price?"

"Well, I guess we could give it a try, and I could talk to the bank about their loan. I know some of those people pretty well. They do a lot of business with Merrill's."

"What did you think of Mary's ideas about the garden?" Laura asked.

"Well, I must admit I am a little intrigued," Ed said. "I hadn't even thought about some of the things she recommended."

"Okay, so why not let Larry come out and make the changes she has recommended?" Laura asked. "While the work is going on, she will be coming out here to check on progress. We can get better acquainted, and I will figure out how to get Troy to come out with her so we can spend a little time together. If we can put our relationship on a friendship basis, we can socialize with them. Then we can decide how to present them with the idea of building here."

On Monday morning Laura called Larry. "Larry, could you have Mary drop off her sketches and the estimate at our house this evening?"

"Sure, she's finishing them up right now."

"That sounds good," she said. "I really appreciate your help on this, and please don't say anything to Mary about what we discussed the other day."

Larry said, "My lips are sealed, but if I can help with whatever you're cooking up, you let me know. What I owe to you guys can't be repaid in money."

"You don't owe us anything, Larry. Without your help Ed would still be studying a pile of stone trying to figure out how to make it look like a wall."

He laughed and said, "Okay, but keep me in mind and let me know if I can help."

"You've got it," she said.

That evening Ed and Laura made sure they were both home when Mary arrived. The weather was nice, so they went over her plans out on the patio. Laura had fixed a few appetizers, and they sat and talked about her ideas. They told her they thought everything looked good and to put them on the schedule. Mary said that she thought they could start on it next week.

As the work progressed, Mary dropped by almost every day to check on progress. Laura made a point of talking to her about the job, her children, and Troy. When everything was finished, Laura asked Mary and Troy to come out on Saturday for lunch on the patio. When Mary told Troy where they were going, he was surprised at his feelings. He had thought several times about meeting Ed. The idea of being able to talk to him again aroused his curiosity. On Saturday they all sat around and talked about how well the garden had turned out. Ed and Troy talked about business and how things were going in their respective careers.

Finally Ed said, "Mary told us you guys were looking for somewhere to build outside of Granville."

Troy said, "Yes, we would love to, but we haven't really looked too much. The kind of land we would like is just too expensive. We thought we would save money for a few years, and then we could buy what we wanted."

Ed said, "Laura and I have been thinking about selling this ten acres next to us, if you would be interested."

Troy looked surprised. "Why would you sell this acreage? It's beautiful and we would love to have it, but we just can't afford it," he said.

Ed laughed and said, "You're right—it is beautiful, but from a practical standpoint it isn't really profitable. We cash-rent it to a local farmer, but a lot of years what it earns hardly pays the taxes on it. We could sell it and put the money somewhere else where it could earn something."

Troy was interested. "I would love to have it, but I have talked to the bank about buying property, and they have been reluctant to loan money for farm acreage," he said. Ed told him what they would sell it to him for. Troy was surprised. "That is a really a good price; surely you could get more for it on the open market," he said.

Ed said, "We probably could, but then we would pay the realtor's commission and we wouldn't know whom we were selling to. Why don't you go by and talk to the bank again about this acreage. Have them call me if they have any questions, and we'll see what develops."

Ed and Laura sat down with Eli and Liz on Sunday to let them know that they were planning to sell the acreage next to them. The kids were surprised that they would let someone build right next to them. Eli asked, "What brought this on?" Laura explained how they had met Mary and Troy and learned of their search for a new place to buy or build. She told them that she and Ed had talked about it and decided to offer to sell them the land. The consensus of opinion of the kids was that if that was what they wanted to do, it was all right with them.

When Troy talked to the loan officer about getting the loan, the loan officer said, "You need to get a survey for us, but I know what that ground looks like, and I would be surprised if we couldn't give you the loan for it. If you can really get it for that price, it would be a real good investment." Troy couldn't wait for Mary to get home so he could tell her. This was something they had been dreaming of for several years now. When Troy had left, the loan officer had to smile. Ed Williams had contacted him that morning to let him know that he would guarantee the loan. But Troy and Mary were not to know about it. Ed and Laura were good customers of the bank, and if that was what they wanted, that is what they would get.

CHAPTER

37

Carolyn dropped Sarah off at day care and took the elevator down to Shipping for her first full day on the job at Merrill's. Gary Hunt was the department head, and he had introduced her to his secretary, Helen, when Laura had brought her down to meet Gary. Helen was in her sixties and was ready to retire and spend some time with her great-grandchildren. She was very friendly and talked to Carolyn about Sarah and how sorry she was about Carolyn's husband dying so young. She told Carolyn all about her family and the plans she and her husband had for when she was retired. By the end of the day Carolyn was amazed at how much she had learned about the job while they were talking about other things. Helen talked to her about the other employees in the department and introduced them when they came by the office during the day.

When she was picking up Sarah at the end of the day, she met Liz, who was picking up Elly. They talked for a while, and when Carolyn was on her way home, she thought about how easy Liz was to talk to. She felt like she had found a friend. When she thought about the last couple of days, she was at a loss to understand how all this could have happened so quickly. She had been at the end of all hope only seventy-two hours ago, and now she could see a whole new world opening up before her.

CHAPTER

38

Two weeks later Laura was talking to Liz about Elly and how she was getting along in the day-care center. Liz said, "She loves it there, and she has met another girl about her age, and they seem to have struck up a friendship."

"What is her name?" Laura asked.

"Her name is Sarah Ingraham," Liz said.

Laura said, "I know her. I met her and her mother, Carolyn, at Merrill's when she came to work on her first day."

"Well, Elly can't talk about anything else. They seem to have hit it off pretty well."

"I'm glad to see her making friends," Laura said. "Maybe you should invite Sarah to Elly's birthday party next month."

Liz laughed. "Elly has already put her on the list."

The week of the party, Ed met Carolyn in day care, and they were watching the girls. Carolyn said, "I'm afraid we won't be able to make it to Elly's party."

Ed said, "I'm sorry. Elly's going to be so disappointed. She was so looking forward to Sarah being there."

"Well, it's just that we don't have any way to get there. I'm afraid the buses don't run out that far," Carolyn said.

Ed thought for a minute. "Could you come if I sent Eli in to pick you up?"

Carolyn paused. "That is just too much trouble. Someone would have to bring us back home. I think we will just have to pass."

It was Ed's turn to pause, and then he said, "I'll tell you what. Eli can pick you up, and you can pack enough clothes for the weekend and ride back with us to work on Monday."

Carolyn was at a loss for what to say. "That is awfully nice of you, but it is such an imposition. I couldn't put you out like that."

"Not at all. It's all settled. We are glad to have you, and Elly and Sarah will love it."

Carolyn was at a loss for words, but she finally nodded and said, "Okay, but you had better run this by Laura. I don't want to put her out."

"Nonsense," he replied. "She will love having you. It will be a pleasure to have someone young as a guest for a couple of days."

When he told Laura about the conversation, her eyes lit up and she said, "You handled that just right. I've got some ideas I want to plant in her head while she's here."

Ed grinned and looked at her and said, "I think I see some conniving going on here. You are devious, do you know that?"

She gave him a hug and said, "You have no idea. Now I need to talk to Liz about my plans."

On Saturday morning when Carolyn and Sarah arrived, Laura took them upstairs and showed them their room. "You just make yourselves at home. Your bathroom is right through that door, and if you need anything, you just let us know." Sarah immediately headed downstairs with Laura to find Elly. Carolyn stood there alone for a few minutes and then sat down and tried to sort out her feelings. She had never felt this way before. She hardly knew these people, and yet she felt close to them. She finally decided it was just that they were so friendly and had been so kind to her and Sarah. But in the back of her mind there was still something she couldn't quite put her finger on.

She walked downstairs and found Laura on the patio getting everything ready for the party. "What can I do to help?" she asked.

"Oh, thank you," Laura said. "You can help me set the table if you want." They arranged everything while they talked about their families and work. When they sat down to talk, Liz came over with food and cake and all the games the kids would be playing. They all sat and talked about everything and nothing. It was just sort of a feeling-out of everyone.

Carolyn sat looking out over the garden and the river below. Beyond the river were fields and farms on the other side of the valley. The beauty of the place was almost like a travel brochure. She said, "Laura, this is the most beautiful place I have ever seen. I don't know how you can stand to leave it even to go to work."

Laura explained how Ed's father and mother had given them the land, and they had built there when the kids were small. Over the years they just kept making improvements. It was sort of a hobby with them.

She explained that they had given ten acres to Liz and Robert when they were ready to build. Then they had met Troy and Mary and had sold them ten acres on the other side. "You will be meeting the Purcells later when they come over with their kids. I think you have met Robert at Merrill's. You will probably know some of the others that work with Ed who will be here. We are all pretty close. They are like family to us. We hope you will come to feel that way too. You are welcome here anytime you feel the need to get away and relax."

Soon the arrivals began, and Carolyn began to relax. She knew most of the people from work, and the ones she didn't know were as friendly as they could be. When she was introduced to Troy and Mary, they asked her if she had been down to the river. She said, "No," so they walked down with her to show her what Ed, Robert, and Troy had done with the picnic area. Carolyn found herself wishing she never had to leave. It was just the most perfect place she had ever seen.

Troy asked her where she lived, and when she told him about her apartment, he said, "You need to get a place of your own. There is just no feeling like it. Mary and I fell in love with this place as soon as we saw it, and buying the ground here is the best thing we ever did. We are going to start building next month."

Carolyn said, "I wish I could afford it. I would be here in a heartbeat."

Later, Mary was talking to Laura, and the subject of Carolyn came up. Mary said, "We were talking to her down by the river, and she just seems so nice. It's too bad she can't afford a place of her own. Troy and I know where her apartment building is, and I wouldn't want to raise a child there."

Laura said, "I agree, but I'm not sure what we can do about it. Ed says she is really good at her job, and they are trying to find her a better position at Merrill's. She was overqualified for the job she took in Shipping, but she needed the work, and Ed thought it could lead to something better."

That evening when the guests had left, the family and Carolyn were sitting in the family room talking about the day's activities. Carolyn said, "It's so beautiful here. I was talking to Troy and Mary today, and they are just so nice. Everyone was so friendly. I want to thank you for this weekend; I feel like I'm on vacation."

Laura said, "Sometimes I still feel that way when we get home for the weekend. This place seems to make me relax and just enjoy life. This has been a big day. I think I'm ready to head for bed. Carolyn, we are fairly early risers, but you come down whenever you feel like it in the morning. We usually don't have breakfast until about eight or so on the weekends. If you want something before then, you help yourself."

Carolyn said, "Come on, Sarah. Let's go up with Laura. You and Elly can play tomorrow."

When they had gone up, Ed and Robert stayed to talk for a while. Robert said, "You know, I was looking at Carolyn's resume the other day, and she really is overqualified for what we have her doing down there in shipping."

Ed said, "I know, but at the time it was the only thing we had available, and she was a little desperate. I explained to her that if I saw something better, I would try to move her up at the first opportunity."

Robert said, "Let me talked to Dad. He was telling me last week that Grover is going to take early retirement. We are going to have to start interviewing for a new purchasing agent. If Carolyn is as good as her resume looks, she could handle that job, and we could have her move into that department for training as soon as we can find a replacement for her in Shipping."

Ed said, "Let me know what John says. If he okays it, I will talk to Carolyn to see what she thinks about it. It would mean a promotion and a decent pay raise, so I don't know why she wouldn't jump on it." When Ed went up to bed, Laura was waiting for him. Ed just looked at her and said, "Liz hasn't been talking to Robert about Carolyn, hasn't she? I think I see a plot here."

She gave him a sly look and said, "I don't know what you're talking about. But I think we need to talk about what you are going to do with the ten acres on the other side of Robert and Liz. Now, get ready for bed. My feet are cold."

CHAPTER

39

On Monday morning Ed's first priority was to check on the job description for their purchasing agent and compare it to Carolyn's resume. He thought she might still be a little overqualified. But it would be a promotion, and the pay was considerably higher. She should be able to buy a place of her own if she wanted out of her apartment. The question was how much debt she would be willing to take on. Robert called just before noon and said that his dad was okay with offering the job to Carolyn. His only concern was the same as Robert's and Ed's. She was capable of much more responsibility, but they also wanted to keep her moving up in the company. It was obvious to them that she would be a good asset when the right job opened up in the future.

Ed called Shipping and asked Carolyn to come up as soon as she was free. She couldn't imagine why they would call her up to Ed's office. Ed's secretary told her to go right in; he was expecting her. Ed was noncommittal. When she sat down, he asked her about her job and if everything was going all right. She told him she couldn't be happier with the way things were going. She had no problem with the job. It was pretty easy, and they were really great people to work with. Ed couldn't suppress a smile. He said, "We have a problem that we hope you can help us with."

Carolyn was at a loss for words. She couldn't imagine why he thought she could help them with some problem. "I don't know how much help I can be, but I'll do whatever I can."

Ed said, "Our purchasing agent has asked to take early retirement, and we don't have anyone ready to replace him. We would like to move you into that job as soon as we can find someone to replace you. He will be here until the end of the year, and he can get you trained before he retires. It would mean a promotion and a pretty good raise in pay. What do you think?"

Carolyn was floored. "I don't know anything about purchasing, but I would love to give it a chance if you think I can do it."

Ed said, "I know you can do it. I just wanted to see if you were willing to take it. As soon as we can get someone trained to do your job, we will move you into the new job."

She didn't know what to say. She could only say, "Thank you. You won't be disappointed. Thanks, too, for this weekend. Sarah can't stop talking about it."

"We enjoyed having you; it was our pleasure. Sarah and Elly seemed to really enjoy themselves . . . Okay, we will let you know when to start working in Purchasing. Depending on how quickly your replacement can take over your job, we may have you work half days in each job until you are both ready to do the jobs."

When Carolyn left the office, her mind was reeling. She couldn't believe what an opportunity she was being given. Then she switched to a more practical thought. *We can get out of the apartment and start looking for something better.* Little did she know how many people were thinking about that exact same thing.

Two weeks later Liz invited Sarah out for a weekend with Elly. She asked Carolyn if she would like to come too. Carolyn didn't have to think too long about it. All she could say was "Are you sure?"

Liz laughed and said, "I'm not sure I can keep track of those girls by myself. Maybe the two of us can. Just pack enough things for the weekend, and you can ride out here with Ed and me after work Friday. Then you can just go to work from here on Monday morning."

Ed and Laura had recruited Liz into their little plot to help Carolyn. Liz was all for it, but she also wondered why they were so interested in helping someone they hadn't really known for very long. Then she thought about the Merrill Shelter and all the time and effort Ed and Laura had put into helping people. It made sense to her that they would help someone like Carolyn. She also liked Carolyn and Sarah, and thought about how much the girls seemed to like each other.

As soon as Carolyn walked in the door Friday evening, she had the weirdest feeling. It was like she was coming home. She had to shake herself, and she thought, *How ridiculous; this is only the second time I've even been here.* But she was so comfortable with these people, and it was hard to explain, even to herself. She helped Laura in the kitchen getting dinner ready, and it seemed so natural to her to be here. She just didn't understand what was happening to her. After dinner they sat out on the patio and talked. All the Williamses were there, and she thought, *I feel so comfortable with all of these people, and I'm really an outsider.* She didn't really recognize that the feelings she was having were the feelings of family.

Saturday morning after breakfast she walked down to the river with Ed and Laura. They sat on the benches in the picnic area and talked. After a while Laura looked at Carolyn and said, "Would you like to live here on the river?"

Carolyn was speechless. "I wish I could, but there is no way I could afford to live out here."

Ed said, "What if I can show you a way?"

"I just don't see how that could be possible. I don't have a penny of savings, and even with my new job it would take me years to save enough to even buy the land."

"Well, think about this," Ed said. "Laura and I thought we might just build a house on the ten acres next to Robert and Liz. Then we would be willing to sell it to you on contract. You wouldn't need a loan. You would pay us, and it would be like paying rent. That way, when you do start moving up in the company, you could pay as much as you could afford every month until it was all paid for."

Carolyn was stunned. She started to cry, and Laura hugged her and said, "Just think about it for now. But we would love for you to do it."

Carolyn was totally taken aback by this. *Why,* she thought, *would these people do this for someone they barely knew?* Her life had completely changed since the first day she walked into Merrill Industries for that interview. When she thought back to that day, she knew that it hadn't been just by chance. She ran that interview through her mind over and over. These were the nicest and most generous people she had ever met. She knew they were deeply involved with the community and had helped many people. She just couldn't understand why they would go to so much trouble for her.

That afternoon she walked down to the river alone and sat in the picnic area. Just as she was getting ready to return to the house, Mary walked down the path and sat down and started talking to her. Carolyn asked, "How long have you and Troy known Ed and Laura?"

Mary laughed and said, "We only met them a little over a year ago, but it seems like we have known them forever."

Then Carolyn related the conversation she'd had with Ed and Laura earlier. "I don't know what to do. It is the kindest, most generous thing I have ever heard of, but I feel like I would be placing a burden on them by accepting."

Mary thought for a moment, and then she told the story of how she and Troy had come to buy their land next door to the Williamses'. "It was right out of the blue, but we haven't regretted it a single time. Troy and I have talked many times about how great these people are. We both agree that somehow they treat us as family. My advice to you would be to take them up on their offer. We would be glad to have you as a neighbor, and I'm sure you will come to love these people as we do. We are about ready to build, but we come out here every chance we get, just to be here. Troy is up there right now trying to picture what it is going to look like when we get everything finished." Carolyn felt overwhelmed, but when she got back to the house, she told Laura that if the offer was still open, she would be happy to take them up on it.

Within months the Purcells' house was finished, and Ed and Troy, with the help of Robert Merrill and Eli, were putting the finishing touches on the landscaping. Ed and Laura were talking about how things were working out, and Laura said, "All we need now is for Eli to get finished with his master's degree and get settled."

Ed sat quietly for a few minutes; then he looked at Laura and said, "I don't think we have to worry about him. I have set aside the acreage next to Carolyn for him when the time comes that he is ready to build. That is, if he wants to live here. Who knows? He may have ideas of his own when he finishes his education."

These were the good years for the Williams family. Troy and Mary and Carolyn all thought of each other as family, even though they were not biologically related. They had family get-togethers and occasionally family vacations. They all followed Ed and Laura's lead when it came to the local community. They gave of their time and money to help with the various projects that came along. The Merrill Shelter was known throughout the country for the way it seemed to move its clients from the streets into productive lives. Carolyn became the go-to person at Merrill Industries for times when problems arose. She flourished under the workload. Sarah and Elly became nearly inseparable as they grew up.

CHAPTER

40

Laura awakened in terrible pain. She lay for a moment trying to sort out what she was feeling. The pain was intense, centered in her chest. She rolled onto her side intending to get out of bed, trying not to wake Ed. She thought she must have heartburn, but she had never felt anything this intense. When she tried to sit up, she couldn't do it. She dropped back on her side and tried to call Ed's name. She needed help. The only sound she could make was a low moan. She couldn't move. Then she heard a soft voice telling her to relax. She knew that voice, but she couldn't quite place it. Then darkness flowed over her, and the world became completely quiet. There was a total lack of sound or feeling. She heard the voice saying her name again. She roused herself and sat up on the edge of the bed. Then the darkness left, and the light was like the first glow of dawn.

She was shocked to see Gabby standing next to the open gate. He beckoned to her, and she rose and walked to the gate without a word. As if awakening from a dream she realized what was happening. She stopped and looked at Gabby and asked, "Can I have a moment?" Gabby nodded, and she stepped back through the gate into their bedroom. She walked over to the bed and looked at Ed sleeping there. It was a shock to see herself lying next to him. She kissed her fingers and placed them on his lips. He didn't move or show any sign that he had felt her touch.

Then she walked, crying, back through the gate. The gate clicked behind her, and she sat down at the first bench she came to. She sat there in tears, sobbing softly. Gabby put a hand on her shoulder and said, "You have company." She looked up, and there was Elaine walking toward her with several people. She stood, and Elaine put an arm around her and led her over to the people standing there. The tears stopped, and she stood wide-eyed looking at her parents, grandparents, and some family members she had almost forgotten about.

Elaine took her hand and said, "Let's go home." The reality of what had just happened slowly overtook her, and she focused on her family. The sadness that she was feeling began to turn to an overwhelming joy at the realization that she was looking at her family. They were hugging and kissing her and welcoming her to this new existence. She looked at Elaine questioningly. Elaine laughed and said, "Go on home with your parents, and when you feel like talking about it, come and visit me. You can start making decisions about what you wish to do here once you get settled."

CHAPTER

41

Ed woke with a start. He lay listening for what had awakened him. Everything was quiet. Then he saw Elaine standing by the bed. She said, "Ed, Laura is with me. We will be here waiting for you when your time comes." Then she was gone.

He couldn't believe what was happening. He rolled over and nudged Laura. She didn't respond, so he said her name and nudged her again. He put his hand on her arm, and it felt cold. He shook her. There was no response. A feeling of horror ran through him. He jumped out of bed and turned on the lights. He rolled her onto her back. There was no response. He realized she was dead. In his mind he could hear Elaine. *She just wants you to know that she loves you and will be waiting for you when you get to The Garden. We will both be here. I don't know when your time will come, but I don't think it will be long.* Ed was on his knees by the bed holding Laura and weeping uncontrollably. He knew it was only a temporary separation, but the loss was no less painful. When he regained control of himself, he called Liz and told her what had happened.

She couldn't accept what he was telling her. She told him she would be right over. She woke Robert and called 911, and they ran over to Ed and Laura's. They found Ed still by the bed weeping. He was inconsolable. Liz called Eli. Then she phoned Troy and Carolyn. Then the EMTs had arrived and confirmed that Laura was gone. It was determined that she had suffered a massive heart attack. She hadn't had a sick day in her life.

The family couldn't believe the number of people who came to the funeral or sent letters of condolence . . . people they didn't even know. They were people she had helped in the shelter or had had some great effect on their lives. They all had stories of support, or even in some cases gifts of money. The ones who spoke of her at the funeral spoke in hushed tones of their experiences with her. The grief was palpable even in total strangers to the family. Ed lost track of the number of people who related tales of her generosity and how far out of her way she had gone to help them. She was laid to rest in the family plot with Elaine, Michael, and Teresa.

When it was all over, Ed was at a complete loss. Life had given him a second great blow. At first the family thought he was going to go into a depression. They were in for a surprise, though. Ed rebounded in a couple of days. He returned to work with a vengeance. He continued to visit the shelter and walk in the garden. Every day he sat on their bench and thought about Laura. He felt that she was close when he sat there. He liked to think about the time they had spent there together and how many problems they had solved there.

A few weeks after the funeral as he sat in the garden, Elaine came to him. She stayed for quite a while, and when she departed it was clear to him what he was to do. He spent a lot of time with Liz talking to her about the shelter and making sure everything was going well. Liz was asked to take over the shelter. She had worked closely with Laura at the shelter, and she knew what Laura would have wanted done. Ed didn't know when his time would come, but he decided he would just keep doing the things he had been doing all his life.

A few years passed, and Ed began to slow a bit and decided it was time to retire. He was still physically in pretty good shape, but it seemed to take longer for him to figure things out. It was harder to make decisions, and he was making dumb mistakes. He decided he would just spend as much time with the kids as he could, and there were a lot of things he could do to keep busy in his garden. He also wanted to spend some time in the garden at the shelter. Eli had started his career out of state, and he missed seeing him. In retirement he could travel to see him more often.

Ed was working on the picnic area on the river. During the winter he hadn't spent much time there, and it needed a lot of attention. They were having a pretty wet spring, and the river had been up quite a bit. He was picking up limbs and debris that had washed up onto the bank, and was just basically cleaning up. Robert and Troy were going to come down to help, but they were gathering tools and trash bags up at the house.

He heard voices and laughter and looked up the river to see some kids in canoes taking advantage of the swollen river. The current was much faster than normal, and they were moving along at a pretty good pace. They were having a great time, and they smiled and waved as they came toward him. He waved back, and then he noticed something that sent chills down his spine. The river was about two hundred feet wide at this point, and on the opposite side about a hundred feet downstream he could see the water boiling over something submerged. He yelled and pointed. The people in the lead canoe were in the center of the river and shot past without any problem. The second canoe was nearer the opposite bank, and the boy paddling realized what Ed was pointing to. He started trying to turn away from the turbulent water, but he was too late. The canoe hit something submerged and turned sideways to the current. The boy was sitting in the back paddling, and a girl was riding in the middle seat. They were thrown out as the canoe rolled over the submerged obstacle. The boy was thrown into the deeper water and swept on downstream. Ed's first thought was that fortunately they were both wearing life jackets. Then he realized that the girl had disappeared. He could see the boy trying to swim to the bank to come back for the girl, but the current was slowing his progress. Ed could see her forearm sticking above the water, and that she was not being swept farther downstream. Then her hand sank below the surface.

He waited for a second to see if she would surface. Then he kicked off his shoes and dove into the water. He swam as hard as he could to try to reach the other bank before he could be swept past her. He realized he was going to make it just as he hit something under the water. He grabbed at a large root sticking out of the water, and he realized that there were many more roots sticking in all directions below the surface. Evidently a large tree stump had been washed down the river during the winter and had lodged in the rocks and mud. He had to fight to keep his head above water. The water was ice-cold, and it was all he could do to hang on. He could see her hand just below the surface about three feet from him. He let go of the root and immediately slammed into her submerged body. He grabbed at another root with his right hand and threw his left arm around her. He let go with his right hand and locked his arms together around her waist. She had already gone limp, and he knew time was running out. He took a deep breath and slid down her back. Then he hit something solid between them. A large root had slid up between her life jacket and her back. The root she was caught on was two or three inches thick, and the end had been broken off, forming a point. Ed reached around in front of her and tried to find the release on the buckle holding the jacket. He was starting to struggle for air. He tried to pull himself up with the shoulders of the jacket, but the current was too strong. He was beginning to lose consciousness, and his lungs were screaming for air. He felt his feet hitting the root below them, and he twisted his legs sideways and set his feet on the root and heaved with all his might. Just when he thought he was going to have to let go, he felt it snap. They immediately bobbed to the surface, and he reached out to an overhanging limb and pulled them onto the bank. He climbed out of the water and pulled the girl onto the bank and started CPR.

Then the pain hit him in the chest like a sledgehammer. He curled up in pain and rolled onto his back gasping for air.

Robert and Troy had reached the picnic area just as Ed reached the girl. They both dove in and swam for the opposite bank. They made it while they were still upstream of the stump. They ran along the bank and got there just as Ed rolled over. Robert resumed CPR on the girl, and Troy knelt beside Ed and tried to get him to sit up and tell him what he needed. Ed looked at Troy and tried to tell him he thought it was his heart. The pain was too great. He closed his eyes and gritted his teeth, hoping the pain would abate. Troy was beginning to blur, and he couldn't focus. Then miraculously the pain stopped. He relaxed and just tried to rest. When he felt like he could get up, he stood and turned to see if he could help.

He staggered back. He was looking at himself lying there in the weeds. Troy was saying something to Robert, but Robert was still trying to revive the girl. Suddenly she coughed and started to cry. They sat her up and tried to calm her. Then Robert looked over to Ed, and the realization slapped him in the face. He tried to administer CPR, but he could get no response. Troy looked across the river and saw Mary walking down the path. He yelled, and she ran to the water's edge. He yelled at her to call 911. She turned and ran back up the path.

By the time help could arrive, it was all over. The girl's boyfriend had run back along the riverbank and was holding her. Robert looked at Troy and shook his head. They were both numb with grief.

CHAPTER

42

Ed heard his name being called. He turned to see Gabby standing by the gate. He looked back at the scene on the riverbank and then turned and walked into The Garden. He felt as if he were walking through water. He felt a resistance to every move he made. He didn't feel the cold sensation he had felt in his previous entries into The Garden. In a few steps the sensation ended, and he felt completely comfortable and at ease. He was looking back at the scene on the river, feeling at a loss as to what he could have done differently.

He became aware of a sound he hadn't noticed before. When he started listening, he realized it was a dog barking in the distance. Gabby put a hand on his shoulder and said, "We've been waiting for you." Then Ed saw a flash of color tearing around the curve of the pathway. It was Curly running for all he was worth. Ed stopped and knelt down, and Curly almost bowled him over as he jumped into his arms.

Then through the tears in his eyes he saw his parents coming down the path. He had to look twice. They looked younger than he could ever remember them. They were both teary-eyed. He didn't think they were ever going to let go of him. The feeling of being able to hold them was indescribable. They both looked like they were in their twenties. When he let go and stepped back, Laura and Elaine were coming down the path to him. They both hugged him and looked back up the path to where the rest of Ed's family stood waiting.

Ed looked back toward the gate and could see the scene there on the riverbank. He felt at once a feeling of great loss and a feeling of incredible freedom. "Who was that girl?" he asked.

"Just a girl," Elaine answered. "It wasn't her time, and you have given her the only thing one's parents are normally capable of giving—life."

Ed walked along the path with his arms around his mother and father. They were all asking questions and bringing each other up to date on their lives. They all went to Elaine and Laura's home and went out on the patio. Elaine and Laura stood with Ed watching the celebration. Curly stayed as close to Ed as he could for the rest of the day.

When all the guests had left, Ed sat and talked to Elaine and Laura about his day. Curly lay at his feet in total contentment. Elaine sat for a few minutes, and then she said, "I don't know what you are expecting now, but I think we should take some time to get comfortable with the situation. Let's just live here together for a few days, and then we will have a better feel for how this is going to work. Can you do that?"

"Actually," he replied, "I think I would be more comfortable with that. I am really out of my depth here. Is this something that you and Laura have talked about?"

Laura said, "Yes, we have talked about it several times, and we both agreed this would be the way to proceed. We are both comfortable with what our future is going to be like, I think. But we are both a little unsure of how to handle it."

Elaine said, "This isn't an unusual situation in The Garden. There are a lot of people who are living with multiple spouses. Each situation is different, but Laura and I are really close, and we are in agreement that we think it will work well for the three of us."

Ed wasn't too sure. He tried to put himself in their position, and he couldn't imagine sharing either one of them with anyone else. But they were right. He could see the wisdom of letting things work themselves out. He took both of them in his arms and hugged them until they gave him kisses on his cheeks. Elaine said, "We've all had a big day. Let's just sit here and talk and watch the sunset. Tomorrow is the first day of our new lives."

CHAPTER

43

Ed was buried next to Laura, Elaine, Michael, and Teresa. Carolyn was standing next to Liz at the graveside service. As she looked at the headstones, she suddenly had a feeling that she couldn't understand. Her feelings were much deeper than she could explain. As she looked at the names on the headstones, her feelings of loss seemed to be much greater than just the loss of Ed and Laura. She had heard the story about Ed's first marriage and the tragedy that had befallen them. She had felt a great sadness when she first heard the story, but anyone who knew Ed would feel the same. Now as she stood there, she had the same feeling of incredible sadness for Elaine and the children. It was as if she had lost close friends but hadn't found out about it until years after their deaths.

She tried to shake off the feeling, but even after they had returned home she still had this strange feeling of loss that she couldn't attribute to Ed alone. A few feet away Troy had a similar experience. He just couldn't quite understand why he was feeling so close to people he had never met. At first he had just been grieving over the loss of Ed, but he realized his feelings also extended to Elaine, Michael, and Teresa. It had been such a tragedy. But it felt personal somehow.

A few days after the funeral there was an announcement in the newspaper that the Merrill Homeless Shelter would now be named The Ed and Laura Williams Shelter of Hope. John Merrill said in the article that Ed and Laura had personally transformed the shelter into something that would benefit the entire community for all future generations.

CHAPTER

44

John Merrill asked Liz if she would continue to run the shelter.? She couldn't imagine not running it. She found that she was drawn almost daily to Ed and Laura's favorite bench in the garden. She would sit there and reminisce, and somehow she felt as if they were there.

A week after the funeral Carolyn went to Ed and Laura's home with Liz to help her clean out closets and help with some housework. Liz and Eli had agreed that when the estate was settled, he would get the house. He knew that he would never be happy living anywhere else.

Liz was going through things in Ed and Laura's closet when she came across the old photographs of Elaine, Ed, and the kids. She called Carolyn to come and see them. As Carolyn was going through the photos, she felt light-headed. She set them down and looked at Liz. She tried to shake off the feeling that she might pass out. She turned pale and had to sit down. Liz took her by the hand and asked her if she was all right. Carolyn asked for her to just give her a minute. Then she looked at Liz and said, "All of these people look familiar to me. I don't understand it. I could never have seen any of these people before, but I feel like I know them. Here is a picture of Michael and Teresa, and their grandparents are standing behind them, and they look familiar also. This is such a weird feeling, and I can't account for it."

Liz said, "Let's go down and have lunch and rest a bit. Maybe you will feel better."

Carolyn couldn't think about anything but the pictures. She searched her mind for something that would tell her why everyone in the pictures seemed so familiar. She just couldn't find the answer. She finally had to let it go. She thought it just had to be the fact that she had been so close to Ed and Laura and her grief was just too deep. Finally she looked at Liz and smiled. She said, "I guess I was just a little overcome by seeing the photos of Ed and Elaine. Until now it wasn't real to me; it was just a tragic story."

CHAPTER

45

Later, Liz sat looking at the pictures, wondering what had upset Carolyn so. She thought about Elaine and her dad and Michael and Teresa. Somewhere in the back of her mind she thought she finally knew the secret. She walked down to her old playhouse in the garden and sat thinking about how extraordinary her parents' lives had been. She thought about her own childhood and how special it had been.

From the time they moved into the river house, she had loved being there. She was forbidden to go near the river, but as she grew older and became more adventurous, she would go down and walk the riverbank looking for arrowheads. She got into a lot of trouble at first, but then Ed took her for swimming lessons, and once Ed and Laura were convinced that she could take care of herself, they let her go to the river. She always had to ask permission, and usually one of them went with her. Being a big sister, though, she would not let Eli go down there alone. She always watched over him.

She remembered when she would drag poor Eli down to the playhouse with her. He was always good about it when she wanted to play the mother and he was the little kid. But then she got a new doll, and that took some of the load off Eli because they could pretend that the doll was the little kid.

She couldn't remember when she first became aware of Elaine. She went from pretending to be the mother to being her helper. Gradually Elaine became more real to her. At first she was just a figment of the imagination, someone she just talked to as she played. Then she began to visualize her. At some point she became real to her. She didn't think of her as Mommy anymore, because she didn't look like Mommy and she told

Liz that her name was Elaine. It was Elaine who first called her doll Elly, and Liz thought that sounded just right. She never doubted that Elly was just short for Elaine.

It was a while before she realized that Eli was responding to Elaine also. Elaine told them she was a secret friend and that only the three of them should know about her. Liz and Eli liked the idea of having their own secret friend. Elaine wasn't always there when they were at the playhouse, but she would always explain when she had been away that she'd had somewhere else she had to be. As the children got a little older, she was there less often, and then finally she stopped coming.

As Liz sat there remembering those days, Eli wandered down from the house, and she told him what she had been thinking about. Then she told him about Carolyn's reaction to the pictures of Ed, Elaine, Michael, and Teresa. She told him what she was thinking about Troy and Carolyn. He looked a little skeptical. They sat there talking about when Elaine had been there.

Then Liz got that old feeling she'd had when she was a young girl. She was starting to ask Eli if he felt it too, when Elaine said, "Hello, guys. It's been a long time, hasn't it?"

Liz and Eli turned, and Elaine was standing there looking just as they had remembered her. Behind her was a beautiful stone wall with a gate in the center. Liz didn't quite know what to say. Then she asked, "How are Mom and Dad?"

"Everyone is fine, dear. I just needed to talk to you about Troy and Carolyn. I want to ask you to never reveal what you suspected today when you were looking at the photographs. I will tell you that you are right. You should also know that Troy is Michael, but they must never know. They will understand when the time comes for them to enter The Garden. At that point they will remember their previous lives. Now I am sure you can understand a lot of things about why Ed and Laura were so close to Troy and Carolyn."

Liz wept softly and then said, "No one will ever know, and I want you to tell Mom and Dad that I will look at them as family from now on."

When Eli could find his voice, he said, "The secret is safe with me. I'll never tell a soul."

Elaine smiled and said, "I knew you would understand. This is the last time you will see me, but if you ever need me, know that I will be aware of your need and do what I can. Take care of each other." Then she was gone. A teary-eyed Liz and Eli hugged and carried the secret for the rest of their lives.

EPILOGUE

Gabby carried an armload of sticks to his fire and brewed another pot of coffee. There would be a few people dropping by under the bridge, and he was always prepared. As he went about his work, he thought about Elaine. He had never had children of his own, and he loved her like a daughter. From the day he had opened the gate for her and the children, he had known she was special. He still visited with her and Ed and Laura from time to time. In all the time he had been the gatekeeper, he had never been this close to anyone. There was something special about them. He smiled to himself at the thought that one by one, generation after generation, their progeny would come to his gate. They always came with the look of surprise or shock . . . sometimes with terrible regret about those they were leaving behind. They soon realized that they were about to see those who had gone before them. They began to understand that sorrow was about to turn to the greatest joy. Gabby thought about the garden that Ed had built at the shelter. The people of Granville had missed something amazing about it. They hadn't noticed that the garden wall at the shelter never needed maintenance. It looked the same way it had looked the day that Ed and Larry had finished it. There was no graffiti on it and no signs of wear, and at the end of the path where Ed and Laura had liked to sit, hidden behind the shrubbery, was a stone that only Ed and Larry knew about. On that stone carefully and lovingly chiseled were two simple words: "Elaine's Wall."